THE
LITTLE
BOOK
OF
RATHMINES

MAURICE CURTIS

The
History
Press
Ireland

First published 2019

The History Press
The Mill, Brimscombe Port
Stroud, Gloucestershire, GL5 2QG
www.thehistorypress.co.uk

British Library Cataloguing in Publication Data.
A catalogue record for this book is available from the British Library.

ISBN 978 0 7509 8696 0

Typesetting and origination by The History Press
Printed and bound in Great Britain by TJ International Ltd.

CONTENTS

ABOUT THE AUTHOR

Maurice Curtis is an historian and prolific author of over fifteen Irish and local history titles, including *Rathmines in Old Photographs* and *The Little Book of Ranelagh*.

ACKNOWLEDGEMENTS

This book might not have been written except for the ground-breaking and sterling work of the late Deirdre Kelly, local historian par excellence and author of *Four Roads to Dublin*. And likewise, with Éamonn MacThomáis, a former Rathmines resident, whose reminiscences on Dublin in the 'rare aul times' were and continue to be an inspiration. Many thanks to Elizabeth Smith for her history of Belgrave Square. We also owe a debt of gratitude to Séamas O'Maitiú and his book, *Dublin's Suburban Towns 1834–1930*. Rathmines Library and Dublin City Libraries Archives are an indispensable and helpful resource. Canon Pat Comerford and his blog constantly provide inspiring insights on many aspects of Dublin and its heritage, including Rathmines. He is forever rambling around his beloved city, camera in hand, and subsequently provides insightful comments including those on Lafcadio Hearn and Leinster Square. Charlie Chawke, owner of the landmark Dropping Well Pub, and his staff, were of great help with the history of the renowned establishment. Donal Fallon and his Comeheretome website on local history is always a mine of information as is another site, Dublinforums.net.

Rathmines Initiative has done much (e.g. Development Plan with DCC) to focus attention on improving the area and for reminding us of its august history and heritage, as with the RRR History Society. The R & R Musical Society celebrated its centenary in 2013 and was a beacon of light. Thanks to George P. Kearns for his photos and reminiscences on 'The Prinner' cinema. Bob Young, aka 'Bongo', a former resident of Mount Pleasant Buildings was a mine of information. Murrough

MacDevitt and Garret O'Brien of the Leinster Cricket Club were helpful. Thanks also to St Mary's Rugby Club; Joseph E.A. Connell for his very useful book *Dublin Rising 1916*; the Glasnevin Trust for information on Nora Connolly O'Brien; the Kenilworth Bowling Club; Stratford LTC; Rathmines Catholic Church; including the Parish Priest, Fr King, the Parish Council, the very knowledgeable organist, John Hughes; and in particular the hard-working and very helpful Parish Secretary, Mary Ryan; the Holy Trinity Church; Grosvenor Road Baptist Church; Rathmines Gospel Church – all were indispensable in my research. Gratitude also to John Byrne of Politico.ie for his interview with Mike Murphy. Finally, a special thanks to all the local (and in particular the long-established family-run) businesses and the helpful past and present residents of Rathmines.

INTRODUCTION

Situated 3km south of the city centre, the village of Rathmines has been a thriving suburb of Dublin since the mid-nineteenth century. Walking from town, Rathmines begins at the leafy Portobello Bridge, and extends to the borders of Ranelagh to the east, Rathgar to the south, and Harold's Cross to the west. The area has long been popular with the well-to-do; in its early days it attracted the wealthy and influential, who sought more salubrious surroundings than the city centre, where poverty and destitution were rife, having been exacerbated by the devastating effects of the Great Famine.

Nowadays, Rathmines is a bustling melting pot – a vibrant community full of contrasts: the centre of the village has a wealth of bars, cafés, restaurants and shops; there are quiet Victorian terraces and modern apartments; there is a healthy mix of family homes, student accommodation and social housing; and there is culture aplenty, with a Town Hall, the excellent Carnegie Library, and state-of-the-art cinemas, all watched over by the unmistakable green dome of the Rathmines parish church.

For decades, Rathmines has been known for the diversity of its population. It is a popular destination for people who are new to Dublin – students and workers from all across Ireland and beyond – who live alongside older residents, many of whom have been in the suburb all their lives. These days, it is a joy to see such a variety of neighbours, with workers from all over the world raising their families here.

DRACULA, THE SINGING PRIEST AND LORD LONGFORD

A feature of Rathmines is the number of prominent individuals in Irish life who lived or were associated with the area and who had an influence in one way or another on Irish history, politics, literature, science, art and society. These include William Temple, Oliver Cromwell, Daniel O'Connell, Robert Emmet, Séan Lemass, Garret Fitzgerald, John Mitchel the Young Irelander, James Stephens the Fenian leader, Michael Collins, Cathal Brugha, the Yeats, Joyce and Osborne families, Countess Markievicz, Lord Longford, Mamie Caden, George Russell (AE), the Gifford sisters, Bram Stoker's wife, the 'Singing Priest', Dr Kathleen Lynn, Annie M.P. Smithson, Dora Sigerson, and many more. It was, and still is, a much sought-after area, and it has also become the home for famous people in politics, the media, the business world, the entertainment and music world, the arts, literature and academia, amongst others. It has also retained its cosmopolitan atmosphere.

THE MAGNIFICENT DOME AND THE CURVED BESSBOROUGH PARADE

Rathmines is blessed with fine buildings and architecture which contribute enormously to the uniqueness and attractiveness of the area. The green-domed Church of Our Lady of Refuge, Rathmines Library, the Town Hall, the Bank of Ireland, the former Belfast Bank/TSB facing the side entrance to Slattery's Pub, the Post Office, the Kodak building, the old YMCA building, Kensington Lodge, the Mageough Home, Grand Canal House, the former College of Commerce (now music school) and other fine buildings in the area, catch a visitor's attention. The fine stained-glass-windowed church with its modern green roof in the grounds of St Louis High School in Charleville Road is another hidden gem. The curved terrace of houses at Bessborough Parade, lying in the shadow of the magnificent dome of Rathmines Catholic Church, is a similar treasure worth noting. Then there are the impressive squares and roads replete with splendid villas, detached red-bricks with granite steps sweeping up to the entrances, and much, much more. All these are a significant architectural heritage that adds to its unique and distinctive character.

FROM THE TOWN HALL TO THE DUBLIN MOUNTAINS

Designed by renowned Irish architect Sir Thomas Drew, Rathmines Town Hall was completed in 1899, making it one of the most impressive nineteenth-century town halls in Dublin. Its clock tower is something of a southside landmark; visible for miles, it punctuates what is already a grand skyline. There is something special about the view from Portobello Bridge to Rathmines, with the Dublin Mountains rolling across the horizon.

1

EARLY HISTORY AND BLOODY FIELDS

THE RATH OF THE CELTS AND THE WRATH OF THE NORMANS

'Rath' is a significant part of the name Rathmines and it gives us some indication of its early history. A 'rath' was a fort or a defensive structure built on an elevated level to protect farms or dwellings. Because of the Gaelic roots of the name, however, it would indicate that the local Irish chieftains, before the coming of the Normans, would have recognised the importance and significance of an elevated location. With the Norman invasion of the late twelfth century, lands near the old city of Dublin were granted to William de Meones, and the area became known as Rath of Meones and subsequently over time evolved into the present-day Rathmines.

CULLENSWOOD AND UPPERCROSS

The history of Rathmines stretches back centuries. Modern-day Rathmines and the surrounding area was once part of ecclesiastical lands known as 'Cuala', 'Cuallu' or 'Cuallan'. In the local surveys of 1326, Cuallu is noted as part of the manor of St Sepulchre. This was the estate, or 'liberty' of the Archbishop of Dublin (and it from here that the colourful Liberties area of Dublin takes its name). Cuallu later became the parish of Cullenswood, a name still extant in many parts of Rathmines and surrounding environs (particularly in neighbouring Ranelagh). Later, Rathmines was included as part of the Barony of Uppercross, a name that has remained in use in Upper Rathmines for generations . The name survives with the Uppercross House Hotel on Rathmines Road just beyond the Post Office. The name Cullenswood also survives in the adjacent suburb of Ranelagh.

THE COURSE OF IRISH HISTORY MIGHT WELL HAVE BEEN DIFFERENT

On 2 August 1649, the area we now know as Rathmines was the site of an intense, bloody battle of lasting political significance. This was during the Eleven Years' War, and the skirmish, between the English Parliamentarian Army and a combination English Royalist and Irish Confederate Catholic Army, led to the defeat of the latter faction, paving the way for the arrival of Oliver Cromwell. Cromwell and his New Model Army arrived at Ringsend within a matter of days, and within four years he had completed his conquest of Ireland.

ENGLISH HAD LIMITED INFLUENCE AND CONTROL IN IRELAND

The Irish Rebellion having begun in 1641, the country had already been at war for eight years by this time. The Irish Catholic Confederation governed most of Ireland from its base in Kilkenny, and had, by 1649, aligned themselves with the Royalists in the English Civil War. The Royalists were opposing the English Parliament, which was determined to reconquer Ireland and destroy its autonomous identity. This included, among other highly contentious issues, suppressing Catholicism and destroying the indigenous land-owning class. Unsurprisingly, becoming allies with any English element was a very controversial proposal, but after a great deal of dispute, the Confederates signed a peace treaty with Charles I. It was agreed that the Confederation would accept Royalist troops and even put their own soldiers under the command of their officers (most notably James Butler, 1st Duke of Ormonde). As the Battle of Rathmines loomed, the English Parliament only held two small enclaves, one in Dublin and one in Derry. Everything was looking positive for the Confederate and Royalist coalition, until in-fighting caused them to take their eye off the ball. A fatal mistake.

SURPRISE: THE ESSENCE OF ATTACK WINS THE BATTLE

The English Parliamentarians had established a garrison in Dublin in 1647, and in July 1649, the 1st Duke of Ormond marched his troops to the southern outskirts of the city, determined to reclaim it for the coalition. The army, comprising 11,000 soldiers, took Rathfarnham Castle, and set up camp close to what is now Palmerstown Park. At that time, the stretch between the camp and the city was open countryside (a sight that is difficult to imagine these days). Slowly, Ormonde inched his army towards the city, repossessing the small satellite villages as they advanced. Confident with his progress, he sent a detachment to occupy the ruined castle at Baggotsrath (now the site of Baggot Street Bridge), unsuspecting that his adversary Michael Jones, the Parliamentary commander, had readied a 5,000-strong company for battle. On 2 August, Ormond's men fled Baggotsrath in the face of a surprise attack and returned to the camp with news of this inevitable escalation in hostilities.

ROYALISTS FLEE THROUGH RATHMINES

By the time Ormande and his commanders could react, it was too late. They sent what units they had ready to stall the advance of the Parliamentarians, hoping that this would give them sufficient time to ready a proper army for combat. But these units were no match for Jones's cavalry. Ormonde's men did their best to retreat to Rathmines, but, with the enemy in hot pursuit, they were roundly overcome. The combat continued until the

English Royalist troops mounted a rear-guard action (under the command of Murrough O'Brien, 1st Earl of Inchiquin), which allowed the others to escape. The number of casualties was contested in the aftermath of the battle; Ormonde recorded a loss of fewer than 1,000 men, while Jones claimed to have taken 4,000 soldiers and imprisoned 2,517 more. In his account, only a handful of his troops were killed. Modern historians tend to lean towards the latter.

OLIVER CROMWELL AMAZED

Having lost so many men, and all his supplies, Ormonde withdrew his troops, leaving the way clear for Oliver Cromwell, who referred to the Battle of Rathmines as 'an astonishing mercy' – a sign from God. He landed at Ringsend on 15 August with 15,000 men, determined to accomplish his conquest of Ireland. On the Confederate side there was widespread disillusionment, with many blaming the association with the Royalists for the state of affairs, and Ormonde was subsequently deposed as leader of Irish military.

THE BLEEDING HORSE AND
THE BLOODY FIELDS

The Battle of Rathmines left a lasting impression in the area, and there are clues to be deciphered in many local landmarks. Perhaps the best-known of these is the Bleeding Horse, a very popular pub at the corner of what is now Upper Camden Street. It is said that shortly after the battle ended, an injured horse wandered into the premises, an occurrence that left such an impression on the landlord that he changed the name of the tavern, and it remains 'The Bleeding Horse' to this day. There is also a painting in this landmark pub depicting the bleeding horse. It is one of Dublin's most historic pubs, and has been frequented over the years by literary greats such as James Joyce, Sheridan La Fanu, Oliver St John Gogarty and J.P. Donleavy.

Palmerston Park in Rathmines was the site of part of the battlefield, and for many years was known as the 'Bloody Fields'.

RATHMINES CASTLE AND SARAH PURSER

The present-day Kildare Place School is located in the grounds of what was originally Rathmines Castle. The castle was built *c.*1820 by a Colonel Wynne. It was later owned by John Purser Griffith, Chief Engineer of the Dublin Port and Docks Board. His niece was the famous artist Sarah Purser. Interestingly, though the castle dates from *c.*1820, Taylor's Map of 1816/16 shows a 'Castle' but much closer to the eastern boundary of the grounds. We might surmise that Wynne's castle was inspired by an earlier castle in the grounds. The Church of Ireland Teacher Training College School is also located on the site of the grounds of the castles.

2

ASCENDANCY CONNECTIONS AND TEMPLE TIMES

WHAT'S IN A NAME?

When one considers the names of many of the roads in Rathmines, one gets an inkling of the history of the area. Names such as Palmerston, Temple, Cowper, Windsor, Prince Arthur, Grosvenor, Richmond, Bessborough, Cambridge, York, Maxwell and Belgrave dominate. There is even a Kensington Lodge. Consequently, the emphasis was on England's history, politics and culture and the residents' loyalty to those. One name in particular that stands out not only in the story of Rathmines, but also in the early growth and development of Dublin, and, for that matter, on Irish history from the seventeenth century onwards. That name is 'Temple'.

TEMPLE TIMES, TEMPLE'S BARR AND RATHMINES

The origins of modern-day tourist mecca Temple Bar can be traced back to the late sixteenth century. Sir William Temple was a famous English teacher and philosopher who entered the service of the Lord Deputy of Ireland in 1599. A decade later, now well-established in Dublin, Temple became Provost of Trinity College and Master Chancery of Ireland, and he built his home on the corner of what is now Temple Lane and Temple Bar. 'Bar', coming from 'barr', means the sandbanks created by deposits carried by the flow of the river, and this area, then known as Temple's Barr, has been called Temple Bar ever since. The shoreline was gradually extended and enclosed over subsequent generations, having originally been along a line coinciding with the present thoroughfare that extends from Essex Street, the Temple Bar street and Fleet Street. North of that line became reclaimed land either from the River Liffey or River Poddle.

TEMPLE AND CROMWELL

John Temple, son of William, wrote a 'history' of the 1641 Irish Rebellion with a strongly partisan and sectarian slant, that was to precipitate intense turmoil in the country. *The Irish Rebellion, True and Impartial History* (1644), quickly repackaged as *History of the Irish Rebellion* in 1646, was a wildly heightened version of the conflict and Temple used sensationalist woodcuts depicting the Irish massacring thousands of settlers. This, quite intentionally, inflamed Protestant indignation against the native Irish, and certainly contributed significantly to the severity of the Cromwellian campaign, in which, as we

have read, Rathmines played a prominent role. John Temple's incendiary book was reprinted many times over the ensuing centuries and helped confirm the colonists in their entitlements.

Contemporary illustration showing Oliver Cromwell in Ireland, 1649, for the Battle of Rathmines.

THE CROWN'S NEST AND
THE DOWN SURVEY

It may be argued that his book helped transform subsequent Irish history. Besides John Temple, two other individuals based in Temple Bar, William Crow and William Petty, were to be instrumental in defining the Cromwellian Plantation. The house of the first, known as the 'Crow's Nest' on what is now Crow Street, was where William Petty (infamous for 'Petty's Down Survey') devised the plan for the confiscation of most of the land of Ireland to give to adventurers and fortune seekers. Over the subsequent years, some of this land went to the descendants of William Temple, including land in what is present-day Rathmines.

Later in the seventeenth century, a Sir George Radcliffe built a mansion in the area (in the vicinity of present-day Palmerston Park) and it and the surrounding lands amounted to some 60 acres. In the eighteenth century, the Temple family took over Radcliffe's lands and house. In 1746 the house was leased to William York, a Chief Justice of the Common Pleas. The Temple family consequently had an influence on the subsequent development of Rathmines right up until the present day.

LEPERS AND PALMS – REMEMBERING
PRIME MINISTER PALMERSTON

The mid-nineteenth-century English Prime Minister Lord Palmerston is remembered in the area, as are his family names, Cowper and Temple. For it was by this time that the Cowper Temple family owned much land in the vicinity of what is now Palmerston Road. The Temple family had been ennobled under the title of Palmerston, the title deriving from Palmerston (now called Palmerstown) in Co. Dublin, an area where Lord Palmerston also owned lands. The name Palmerstown (previously Palmerston) derives from the medieval term 'palmer', meaning a pilgrim who has returned from the Holy Land with a piece of palm as a token of their journey. These pilgrims were often associated with leper hospitals, and indeed there was a leper hospital dedicated to St Laurence in the area.

'PAM' AND 'THE MONGOOSE'

Lord Palmerston (Henry John Temple, 1784–1865) was the third and last Viscount Palmerston. He was a Liberal politician, later British Prime Minister, and he spent most of his adult life in government. Popularly referred to as 'Pam' and 'the Mongoose', Lord Palmerston served in office from 1807 until his death in 1865. When this part of Rathmines began to be developed from the mid-nineteenth century onwards, the name Palmerston (and Temple and Cowper) became popularised in the area.

DIAMONDS AND THE COUNTESS

One interesting piece depicting the family dates from the 1860s. The diamond-shaped collage features nine individual studio portraits of the members of the Palmerston family, suggesting family unity, cohesion and permanence. There is a sense of strength, balance and continuity in the image, which is adorned with a cherry-blossom border. It comes from the Jocelyn Album of Countess Cowper. Lady Jocelyn artfully placed her stepfather, Prime Minister Lord Palmerston, at the apex of the piece and her mother, Lady Palmerston, at the base, with their children and grandchildren arranged safely between them.

Diamond-shaped collage of the Palmerston Family. 'Diamond Shape with Nine Studio Portraits of the Palmerston Family and a Painted Cherry Blossom', from the Jocelyn Album, 1860s.

3

FROM OBSCURE VILLAGE TO A FINE SUBURB

THE BOLLARD, THE CHAINS AND THE RAMSHACKLE VILLAGE

In the early nineteenth century, Rathmines was a very green, sparsely populated area, as evidenced in John Taylor's map of the environs of Dublin, 1816. This map shows Portobello Barracks and Rathmines Castle, as well as some houses along the main road. Fast-forward just two decades and there has been a huge amount of development. In the Ordnance Survey map of 1837, one can see new large houses and terraces.

Probably, the early village of Rathmines developed around a tributary of the River Dodder, known as the Swan River, as it flowed through Rathmines. The only reminder today of this

village is an old bollard near the junction of Rathmines Road and Wynnefield Road. The ramshackle village was known locally as 'The Chains' because of chains separating the old cottages from the nearby river.

One of earliest maps of Rathmines and Ranelagh, Taylor's 1816. *Courtesy of UCD Map Library*

In *The Neighbourhood of Dublin: its Topography, Antiquities, and Historical Association* (1912), Weston St John Joyce maintains that 'The Chains' were so called, because a number of dilapidated shanties at this point were enclosed by chains hung from stone pillars such as now surround Stephen's Green. These old rookeries were really an unsightly and insanitary slum, and were swept away some twenty-five years ago, much to the advantage of the neighbourhood.'

THE BARONY OF UPPERCROSS – FINE HOUSES AND SERVANTS

Yet, 'The Chains' was only a part of the growing village of Rathmines. As was the case in the growth of many of Dublin's villages, including the nearby Ranelagh, Rathgar and Rathfarnham, the existence of a fine house helped in the development of a local village to service its needs, whether that be servants or supplies and provisions. Lewis's *Topographical Dictionary of Ireland* (1837) described the growing village as: 'a considerable village and suburb of Dublin in the barony

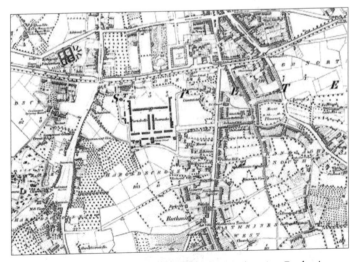

Taylor's map of the environs of Dublin, 1816, showing Rathmines.

of Uppercross, on the old road to Milltown, two miles from the G.P.O. containing 1,600 inhabitants.' Lewis noted that there was 'a station of the city police' located at the corner of Rathmines. There was also a woollen factory owned by Messrs Wilans.

Lewis then pointed out:

> Twelve years since, Rathmines was only known as an obscure village. It now forms a fine suburb, commencing at Portobello Bridge and continuing in a line of handsome houses, with some pretty detached villas, about one mile and a half. [...] Among the most conspicuous are Rathmines Castle, the residence of J.T. Purser, Esq., a castellated mansion in tastefully disposed grounds.

The *Dublin Penny Journal* of 14 September 1833 surmised that while it presented an antiquated appearance, with its round Norman towers connected by curtain walls, its parapets and mullioned windows, its mouldings and machicolations, it was in fact an imitation, the original house having been enlarged and altered by Colonel Wynne.

It survived until the second half of the twentieth century. It was eventually demolished and became the site of the Church of Ireland Teacher Training College and later also of Kildare Place School, which moved from Kildare Place in 1969.

1833 image of Rathmines Castle, Rathmines Road as shown in the *Dublin Penny Journal*.

THE GRATTAN SPA OR A SEWER

For hundreds of years, Rathmines was famous for its spa, or spring, and people came from far and wide to avail themselves of the supposed health benefits of the water there. Located on land close to Grove Park and Portobello Bridge, in the nineteenth century it became known as 'Grattan Spa', because it was situated on land that had belonged to Henry Grattan, the acclaimed politician and orator. Gradually, the spa became neglected and fell into disrepair, and in the 1870s disagreements arose as to whether the spa should be restored for posterity or done away with completely. In a bid to settle the dispute, a local property developer called Frederick Stokes sent samples of the water to Dr Cameron, the medical inspector. His report stated that, 'It was, in all probability, merely the draining of some ancient disused sewer, not a chalybeate spring.' The once-popular spa was swiftly closed to visitors, and it gradually faded from public memory.

HABERDASHERS, BOOTMAKERS AND BAKERS, ALEX FINDLATER AND LEES OF RATHMINES

Thom's Directory during the mid-nineteenth century shows that Rathmines had nine grocers and provision dealers, a post office, chemist, butchers, bakers, bootmakers, wine and spirit dealers, haberdashers, a dairy, builders, painters, glaziers and sundry other businesses. Many of these small businesses were located in the vicinity of the old village.

Over time, bigger city-based shops opened up in Rathmines to cater for the more refined needs of the residents. These included Alex Findlater's grocers and wine merchants; William Magee with similar produce as Findlater's; Hamilton Long, chemists; Gilbey's wine dealers; and the famous Lees of Rathmines shop. Most of these major businesses survived in Rathmines for more than 100 years until the 1970s. Today we are reminded of an early business with the name and date 'The Leinster House, 1843' over the entrance to what later became Madigan's Pub and today Copán's.

Lees of Rathmines was a well-known shop for over 100 years.

THE GREAT FAMINE, TENEMENTS AND THE EXODUS FROM THE CITY

The expansion in business life in Rathmines coincided and was consequent to the fact that Dublin city was, at this time, becoming increasingly polluted and depressed, with tenements everywhere. As a result, and in great haste in the years of and following the Great Famine, the professional and middle classes, and later the lower-middle classes, began to leave the city in droves and move to new housing developments in Rathmines and beyond.

4

THE RATHMINES TOWNSHIP AND THE FOUR-FACED LIAR

SPECULATIVE BUILDERS AND A PROPERTY DEVELOPER'S PARADISE

With this changed horizon leading to the expansion of the new suburb, Mary Daly of the Urban District Council (UDC) noted in her *Victorian Dublin* that 'Rathmines was a property developer's paradise and control was shared by a small number of businessmen who had extensive property interests in the area.'

One of the main developers of the Rathmines and Portobello areas in the nineteenth century was Frederick Stokes. An Englishman, Stokes was the first Chairman of the Rathmines Township Commissioners. To encourage prospective buyers to move to Rathmines from the overcrowded city, rates were kept to a minimum. Consequently, many wealthy residents of the teeming metropolis moved across the Grand Canal to Rathmines.

As time went on, the demand grew for more suburban accommodation for the lower-middle-class groups, and the Rathmines Commissioners were not slow to satisfy the demand. By the end of the nineteenth century, building had moved from fine, wide roads, like Palmerston and Leinster roads, to smaller terraces such as Gulistan.

THE TOWNSHIP AND THE CONSOLIDATION OF RATHMINES

Rathmines became classified as a township in 1847, a development that significantly catalysed the growth of the area, which then had a population of 10,000. Frederick Stokes and his associate Terence Dolan led the campaign to reclassify the area, under the Towns Improvement Act, and a small group of businessmen assumed responsibility for managing the district. Naturally, Frederick Stokes was the first chairman of the Rathmines Township (which later expanded to become 'Rathmines and Rathgar', encompassing Harold's Cross, Ranelagh, Sandymount and Milltown). Most of those on the council had property interests in the area, and so, while the township was initially only responsible for sanitation, the new Rathmines council revised byelaws, building standards and rates to encourage development, both in terms of housing and public amenities.

SCOTCH, SHAMROCKS AND ON TO THE PILLAR

Under the Rathmines Township, much progress was made in developing the area. In 1872, the Tramway from Dublin's O'Connell Street (Nelson's Pillar, known as 'the Pillar', was the terminus) to Rathmines opened. The townships of Rathmines and Pembroke co-operated on a major drainage scheme in the 1880s, and the end of the nineteenth century saw the construction of smaller terraces for lower- and middle-class families (working-class families remained in the minority in the area during this time). Electric street lighting was introduced in 1903, thanks to the opening of the Pigeon House power station in Ringsend, and many of the lamp standards on the main roads featured interesting shamrock motifs.

PIP PIP AND ALL THAT IN RATHMINES – O THE SOLID, QUIET REFINEMENT

Rathmines' image was rapidly becoming solid, bourgeois and red-brick – cosy exclusiveness. This did not happen by accident, as one of the main reasons for the growth of Rathmines in the late nineteenth century was that, according to the historian Séamas O'Maitiú, who wrote on the development of the Dublin townships:

> The Victorians held the strong view that to reinforce middle-class values, social segregation was necessary with the creation of single-class homogenous districts.

Consequently, there would be little room for 'inferior' housing stock in such areas. Many of the early residents would have been senior civil servants and officials in the Dublin Castle administration or public bodies, and prosperous families that built villas.

WIGS, FANS, GRANITE AND COLUMNS

The terraces that were built from the 1830s and 1840s were originally occupied by single, middle-class families, usually with service areas in the basement and stables to the rear. Much of the original nineteenth-century architecture remains, as highlighted in Dublin City Council's *Conservation and Urban Regeneration Study of Lower Rathmines Road* (2005). The following extract describes houses typical of this era situated on Leinster Road:

> The houses are typically two bays wide and three-storey over basement, the entrance elevated by a half level over a rendered basement. The formal entrance doors are flanked by columns or consoles in arched openings with leaded fanlights above. The service entrance is located under the entrance steps.
>
> The upper floors are faced with stock brick ranging from buff to reddish colour. All houses retain their original brickwork

and a good proportion has original 'wigged' pointing of traditional lime mortar. The original windows are six-over-six-paned sliding sash windows at each level, those on the top floor being slightly smaller. The roofs, concealed from view behind a parapet, consist of double-pitched slated roofs with a central valley and flashings of lead. Original rainwater goods are of cast-iron. Front gardens form a semi-private defensible space to the public street, enclosed by decorative railings in a variety of types with granite plinth stones or plinth walls of exposed brickwork, capped with granite.

Typical coach houses to the rear, backing on to Grosvenor Lane [originally called 'Buck's Lane' after Buckley's Orchard in the vicinity] were originally small two-storey structures with simple pitched roofs.

FANLIGHTS, HONEYSUCKLE BOUNDARIES, SWORDS AND SHAMROCKS

The architectural style of the houses in some areas of the township were derived from the typical eighteenth-century Dublin townhouses. Externally, the houses could be considered plain, were it not for the enrichment offered by various architectural features, which add variety and decoration to the otherwise uniform and restrained design. Neoclassical-inspired features such as door cases, porches, fanlights, doorknockers, and in particular ironwork are of great quality and diversity.

The term 'fanlight', coined around 1770, describes the semi-circular over-door window, which had a number of panes radiating like a fan or setting sun design. Besides being functional, they became more decorative and there are quite a number of different styles in Rathmines. Glazing bars, initially made of wood, and later of lead and wrought iron, allowed more flexibility and scope for endless pattern variations.

Many of the fine houses in Rathmines area provide examples of fanlights as a decorative feature. At one stage, manufacturers issued catalogues of patterns. A short stroll from Rathmines

Road via Richmond Hill is Mount Pleasant Square, a hidden gem of a curved late Georgian square, and which provides an opportunity to see many examples of these fanlights, and much else from that era.

FOOT-SCRAPERS AND SPIKE-HEADED RAILINGS

From one end of Rathmines to the other, one can spot an abundance of ornate cast-ironwork: in the railings, the balconies, the foot-scrapers and the streetlights. As we have seen, shamrocks can be spotted on the lamp-heads, but this isn't the only emblem to be found. Look closely at a foot-scraper and you might see a lyre or the honeysuckle.

Foot-scrapers served the most practical of purposes – to clean the muck from one's feet before entering the home, but there was no reason that these could not also be fine aesthetic objects in their own right. Railings often continue the honeysuckle and shamrock motifs, usually contrasted with scrolls and swords, to reflect this ironwork's dual purpose of decoration and defence.

CHIMNEYS AND COAL-HOLES, POST BOXES AND ROYAL CYPHERS

For the interested eye, there is an attractive and historic selection of chimneys, coal-hole covers, post boxes and lamp posts in Rathmines. With the tall soaring chimneys, builders were able to avail themselves of a vast array of clayware pots. Many are examples of the Victorian exuberance for ornamentation with plain pots juxtaposed with the ornate.

The coal-hole covers are an excellent, but often overlooked, examples of cast-iron 'street furniture'. Usually placed on the footpath outside, these hatches allowed coal to be poured into a bunker beneath the house, ready to be retrieved by the staff as required. The covers, which only opened inward for security reasons, were often adorned with arresting designs, ranging from floral to geometric patterns. Some of the most interesting examples can be found around Mount Pleasant Square.

Likewise with post boxes, some bearing the royal cypher of Queen Victoria (VR), King Edward (ER) or King George V box (GR, e.g. outside Fothergill's on Upper Rathmines Road and at Temple Gardens), or P 7 T (Post & Telegraphs) each reflecting a specific era. Victorian wall boxes are also evident in the wider area. The first post box in Ireland was introduced in 1855. With Irish independence, the Post Office changed the colour of the post boxes to green, having originally been red-coloured.

LIFE UPSTAIRS AND DOWNSTAIRS: BEETON'S SERVANTS AND BEATING CARPETS

The vast majority of houses in Rathmines had at least one domestic servant looking after the household's needs. The size of the houses and the social aspirations of the residents necessitated having servants. The number of servants per house varied from one to four. Residents looked to Mrs Beeton's Victorian classic household management book for guidance on the roles and work for the servants. Titles ranged from 'maid-of-all-work' where there was only one servant who did practically everything in the house, to housemaid, parlour maid and cook for the bigger houses.

It was not until the 1920s that the benefits of electricity began to be felt and the need for domestic servants was reappraised. In the meantime, the three- and four-storey houses of the wealthy in Rathmines would have presented a formidable workout for those maids engaged in carrying coals to the fireplaces on the various levels, beating rugs and carpets, and keeping the linen in order. Thousands of domestic servants were employed in Rathmines and the surrounding area and the name given to the new church on Rathgar Road is a testament to this – it was known by the residents as 'the Servants' Church'.

The Lady of the House, 1901.

CANAL WATER OR RIVER DODDER WATER

The township of Rathmines remained under the governance of the commissioners until the Local Government (Ireland) Act of 1898, when the Rathmines and Rathgar Urban District Council was established. Over time, the township became responsible for a wide array of duties, both in terms of local government and public services (such as street lighting and drainage). Rathmines was growing rapidly, and the water supply was struggling to keep up. The township could ask the Dublin Corporation to supply the water, but this would in turn increase the rates, the modest level of which had been a key incentive to live here until this point. It was proposed that water could be taken from the Grand Canal, but this proved impractical, and so Robert Mallet was commissioned to investigate the feasibility of using the River Dodder as a water source. Research commenced around 1844, and in 1872, the township's water tower was built. It was located on a lane off Brighton Road, Rathgar, which is now, unsurprisingly, called Tower Avenue. Water began flowing in 1878.

STUBBORNLY MAINTAINING ITS EXCLUSIVITY – THE FOUR-FACED LIAR

With their increased remit and responsibilities, the Rathmines commissioners felt they needed a place where they could meet and conduct their business. The first 'town hall' was located at 71 Rathmines Road, with the new edifice by Sir Thomas Drew being completed in 1896.

Drew was one of the most distinguished architects of the nineteenth century in Ireland. He was president of the Royal Institute of the Architects of Ireland (RIAI), and he held the Chair of Architecture at the new National University of Ireland. His fine red sandstone and brick edifice was complemented by interior fittings by Carlo Cambi of Siena (whose doors and panelling can also be seen in the National Library and the National Museum of Ireland).

In a building rich with detail, one feature stands out in particular: the clock in the tower. It is often referred to as 'the four-faced liar'; this is because prior to electrification, its four faces often disagreed with one another, showing slight variations on the time. Perhaps the quintessential Rathmines landmark, the prominent clock tower is visible for miles and it continues to stand guard over what is now Rathmines College.

LOYALTY, ROYALTY AND NATIONALIST WRECKS

The new Town Hall opened with great pomp and ceremony. An early image of the Town Hall, taken at its official opening in 1896, shows it festooned with regal decorations, flags and bunting. Today, on the lower base of the clock tower and just over the curved bay window, a reminder of that era is carved into the stone. Beside the ornate lettering RTC (Rathmines Township

Commissioners) the words 'Victoriae' and 'Decimo', relating to Queen Victoria, are visible.

Rathmines then was a strongly Protestant Unionist area with a great attachment to the British monarchy. Forty-six per cent of its population in 1871 was Protestant. The remainder, though Catholic, would have consisted mainly of thousands of live-in domestics and servants. That the area established its own township illustrates its desire to be separate from the encroaching Catholic Irish and nationalist population. The southern Unionists or loyalists had no intention of embracing an Irish identity or associating with the Dublin Corporation, which was seen as a 'dumping ground for Nationalist wrecks' as one prominent developer and Unionist noted. There was no intention of power-sharing with the nationalist population.

MUCH WEEPING AND GNASHING OF UNIONIST TEETH

Loyal addresses to members of the UK royal family were a common feature of local government at this time. In Unionist Rathmines there was never a question of a loyal address being opposed. And when the Town Hall officially opened in 1896 the building was festooned with Queen Victoria royalty decorations. Likewise, across the road, when the new Rathmines Library opened in 1913, a British flag hung over the entrance. There was much weeping and gnashing of teeth with the changes ushered in by the successful fight for Irish independence.

By 1911, the population of the Township had reached 37,840. These were predominantly Protestant and middle class and occupied 7,050 houses.

Rathmines had a Unionist majority up to the late 1920s, when all Dublin borough councils were abolished in the local government re-organisation. The last unionist politician to be elected from the borough was Maurice Dockrell (1850–1929).

'ARE YE RIGHT THERE MICHAEL?'– SINGING WITH VICTORIA AND MARCONI

Apart from the town commissioners' boardroom, concerts, dances and other events were held in the 2,000-capacity hall. One of the regular performers was the great Percy French. Roscommon-born French wrote many well-known, beloved songs, including 'Phil the Fluther's Ball', 'The Mountains of Mourne', 'Come Back Paddy Riley', 'Eileen Oge', and 'Abdul Abulbul Amir', and together with his own theatrical company, he gave many performances in Rathmines Town Hall. Other notables gracing its stage included W.B. Yeats, Lennox Robinson, Liam O'Flaherty and Hanna Sheehy Skeffington. One of the first moving films made by a man called Edison was shown here in 1902. Another of the events that took place here was a demonstration of the wireless telegraphy invention by Marconi.

The Township survived until well into the twentieth century when, under the Local Government (Dublin) Act of 1930, its administration was taken over by Dublin City Council. The Urban District Council (UDC) held its last meeting in the Town Hall in 1930. In 1930, Rathmines Township was incorporated into the City of Dublin. The functions of the

1917 advertisement for Town Hall, Rathmines.

committee were taken over by Dublin Corporation (now Dublin City Council), of which Rathmines remains a local electoral area. The original hall has unfortunately been gutted but the chamber remains intact.

5

TRAMS, BARGES AND THE SWAN

THE SWAN RIVER, THE CHAINS AND THE BOLLARD

The old Rathmines village was a group of thatched houses beside the Swan River as it meandered along by the present-day Wynnefield Road and Rathmines Road. The river, a tributary of the River Dodder, although now mainly hidden from view and culverted, has defined parts of the landscape and topography of Rathmines and Ranelagh. Mount Pleasant Square is an example of this influence and it was designed to take into account the flow of the nearby river. From its source beyond Kimmage Manor, the Swan River flows through Rathmines and Ranelagh, before joining the River Dodder at Ballsbridge. In Ranelagh, it moves east through Mount Pleasant Square into Ranelagh

Gardens. It was culverted over time, but the Swan River is commemorated in a number of place names, including Swan Grove, Swan Place, and the Swan Shopping and Leisure Centres.

Early map of Grand Canal, 1798.

THE GRAND CANAL, THE SHANNON, STOUT AND TURF

The Grand Canal waterway is the northern boundary of Rathmines. The main line runs from Ringsend in Dublin to the Shannon Harbour in County Offaly and is approximately 82 miles long with forty-three locks for barges and other forms of transport. The idea for this canal, to link Dublin with the River Shannon, was first mooted in 1715 and construction commenced in 1756, with most of it (to Tullamore) completed by 1790. The stretch from Portobello Harbour to Ringsend Basin was started in 1790 and was completed in 1796. The last stretch to the Shannon was finished a few years later, with the official opening in 1804. It was a major means of transport for goods and passengers.

The very first trade boat passed from Dublin all the way through to the Shannon in 1804. Typical cargoes would be barrels of Guinness leaving Dublin for rural towns and cargos of turf coming to Dublin to be burnt in urban fireplaces. Although the last working cargo barge made its way through the Grand Canal in 1960, this route remains popular for pleasure-boat trips, and the bank paths are popular for walking, jogging and cycling. It is generally accepted that the Grand Canal marks the southern boundary of Dublin city centre.

Early nineteenth-century view, by Samuel F. Brocas, of Portobello House, La Touche Bridge and Grand Canal. *Courtesy of NLI*

PORTOBELLO HOTEL AND HARBOUR

The Asylum, the Romanists and Fresh Souls to Save

In 1807, a depot for passenger traffic along the Grand Canal was established at Portobello Harbour (the harbour, now covered in, was opened in 1801). Here also, a palatial hotel, The Grand Canal Hotel (facing Rathmines), was erected for the thousands of passengers who were anticipated.The hotel, which was designed by architect James Colbourne, was opened in 1807.

Fifty years passed, but eventually the emergence of other modes of transport (the railway in particular) saw business slow dramatically, and in 1858 the hotel became St Mary's asylum for blind girls. It was operated by Catholic nuns for the next decade, before it was purchased by Isaac Cole, who reverted the building to a hotel once again. Cole's hotel slept 100 people and was popular with personnel visiting the nearby Portobello Barracks. Cole claimed that the hotel was, at that time, the closest one to the RDS, which is hard to believe these days. The twentieth century saw the building transformed again, this time into a nursing home. The Irish painter, Jack B. Yeats spent his last days there, as did Lord Longford.

Early nineteenth-century sketch of LaTouche (or Portobello Bridge) from Rathmines Road. *Courtesy of Dublin Forums*

Jenkin's Ear and the Liberator

Portobello, like its namesakes in the UK, the USA and New Zealand, is named for the Battle of Porto Bello, a 1793 clash between the British Navy and Spanish defenders in Panama. Here, it refers to the area between the South Circular Road and the canal, from north to south, and from east to west from Robert Emmet Bridge at the end of Clanbrassil Street to Portobello Bridge (between South Richmond Street and Rathmines). While this bridge is widely referred to as Portobello Bridge, its official name is La Touche Bridge. It was given the title in honour of William Digges La Touche, a member of a prominent business family and director of the Grand Canal Company. Its unusual name, coined by Thomas Carlyle in 1858, relates to Robert Jenkins, captain of a British merchant ship, who exhibited his severed ear in Parliament following the boarding of his vessel by Spanish coast guards in 1731. This affair and a number of similar incidents sparked a war against the Spanish Empire.

Stuffed Birds and Stockbrokers

Many residents of Rathmines will be familiar with two landmark premises beside Portobello Bridge – Christy Bird's and the Portobello Bar and Hotel. The bar has an interesting history including links with James and Eugene Davy, the brothers who founded the famous firm of stockbrokers of the same name. At the turn of the nineteenth century, the family was associated with a number of pubs including the J.&T. Davy Pub at Portobello Bridge (now the Portobello Bar and Hotel). James had been advised to go into stockbroking by his UCD economics professor. In 1926, he became a member of the Dublin Stock Exchange and was soon joined by his brother Eugene to establish J&E Davy, with its first office located on Westmoreland Street. The brothers built up the business over the next few decades by tapping into the slowly emerging Irish middle class living in new suburbs such as Rathmines and the surrounding area. The Davys were born and raised at 29 Terenure Road East, a short stroll to Rathmines and Portobello Bridge.

THE PAWNBROKER AND THE
OLD BIRD OF PORTOBELLO

Just around the corner from the Portobello Bar is another Dublin landmark – Christy Bird's, a legendary second-hand furniture and antique shop that has helped to furnish most of the bedsits and flats of Rathmines over the years. It all began in 1945, as a 2005 profile in the local *Village Quarter* explains:

> when the manager of the pawnbroker on Charlemount Mall [along the banks of the Grand Canal] retired. He had moved to Dublin from Trim, Co. Meath, in 1908 to take up his apprenticeship ... He finally settled in Upper Lesson Street, where he lived and raised his family over the next forty years ... He had been widowed with a young family at the age of forty-five. So, no one would begrudge him his retirement. But being the man he was, he took his retirement clock, all his savings and bought a shop on South Richmond Street, Portobello. He put the clock in the window, and by selling it he had set up one of Dublin's best-known antique and second-hand furniture shops.

The proprietor proudly put his name above the door: 'CHRISTY BIRD & CO.' As Rathmines locals know, and the *Village Quarter* affirms, 'From that day Christy Bird & Co. has been recycling Dubliners' furniture, be it household or antique, and if it had a resale value they would sell it.'

'On Yer Bike' said Mr Bird to the Recycled Skeleton

In the early years of operation, Christy Bird had the largest selection of second-hand bicycles in Dublin. These were the days after the Second World War, and cycling was the most popular way to travel through the city. Bird held a tremendous number of black bikes, and so his shop was one of the first ports of call for people when they moved to Dublin.

Bird also had a good relationship with students, particularly those attending the College of Surgeons on York Street, just up the road. When scholars completed the part of their studies that required the use of real skeletons, they would sell them to Christy Bird, who in turn would sell them to the next crop of first-year students. With more than a little dark humour, he referred to the practice as 'bare bone recycling'.

An Oscar for Christy

Of course, a treasure trove of artefacts like Christy Bird & Co. is heaven for those in the creative industries. For decades, Dublin's most important theatre companies have hired props from Bird's, and the boom in film production in Ireland has seen many of the shop's pieces transported to the silver screen. Furniture and props from the shop can be seen in, among other hits, *Saving Private Ryan*, *The Field*, *My Left Foot*, *Angela's Ashes*, *The Commitments*, *Cal*, and *Out of Africa*, which won an Academy Award for Production Design. Of course, it doesn't hurt business to be able to boast that a chair for sale was used by Liam Neeson in *Michael Collins* or, closer to home, that a kitchen table used to sit in Miley and Biddy's kitchen in the classic RTÉ programme *Glenroe*.

MONSTERS AND THE LADY OF THE HOUSE

The Horror of Juggernauts

For many years, single-carriage trams and later buses were a feature of public transport in Rathmines and the newer suburbs of Dublin in the late nineteenth century. The old trams, unlike the modern Luas version, used the main roads rather than the railway line. Originally these trams were pulled by horses, but by the

Routes of the DUTC that included Rathmines.

end of the nineteenth century they were electrified. The poet Katherine Tyan, who lived in the area, recalled with horror the early electric trams. In an article, 'Lady of the House', she remembered going to school, and it being very near the main road along which the trams passed. She recalled, 'I remember the first trams, monstrous creatures, coming with a creaking and a groaning over Portobello Bridge and hurling themselves like a juggernaut down Richmond Street.'

Jaunting Cars, Horses and Cyclists

Before the advent of trams to Rathmines, residents used to commute via jaunting cars and hackney carriages in the early decades of the nineteenth century. In later years, horse-riding was popular, but more for social purposes. The *Rathmines and Dublin Lantern* even reported on 'well-known equestrians of the area heading off to Sandymount for a gallop'. Even later still the new fad of cycling took over Rathmines, precipitating an urgent meeting of the Urban District Council following reports of many accidents. At a meeting in 1896 it was agreed that cyclists were more dangerous than horses and henceforth they were to confine their cycling to the Kenilworth Square area.

A Terrible Tragedy at Portobello Bridge

The supremacy of the bicycle came under threat in the mid-nineteenth century with the introduction of the horse-drawn omnibus and the tram. On the route between Rathmines and Dublin city centre, Portobello Bridge caused frequent problems for horses, due to its steep incline. Sadly, it was to lead to tragedy in 1861.

On Saturday, 6 April, at around 9 o'clock at night, having just stopped to let a passenger alight, Patrick Hardy steered his bus towards the bridge. Disaster struck when one of the horses started to rear, proving uncontrollable. Despite Hardy's best efforts, the bus, with its six passengers and its horses, fell back through the wooden railings and into the canal lock below. The conductor had managed to jump out, and a policeman rescued Hardy, but sadly, despite the frenzied efforts of onlookers, all passengers were lost.

In her 1998 book, *Dublin's Victorian Houses*, Mary Daly explains that the repercussions of the tragedy were long-lasting, and that from them on, passengers on horse-drawn buses would get off and walk across the bridge on foot, before boarding the bus again.

Tramyards, Hazards and Diamonds

There were a number of 'stands' in Rathmines and beyond to cater for the needs of the transport system. These stands were also called 'hazards' and one was at the Diamond (junction) opposite the Baptist church on Grosvenor Road. There were strict rules as to the running of these stands or hazards. The horses' heads had to be facing a certain direction, the carriages had to rotate from stand to stand, and the behaviour of the drivers had to be impeccable.

Tram horses wore harnesses trimmed with red and adorned with little bells. 'The inside of the cars', the *Daily Express* noted, 'are richly cushioned in velvet and fitted with sliding shutters of Venetian glass type – the lamps are placed within ornamental coloured plate compartments.' The *Irish Times* was less impressed: 'Only a pair of horses was provided for each tram, and these do not appear to be in breeding or stamina

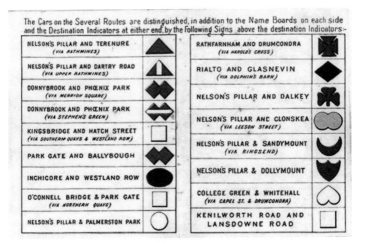

Routes of the DUTC that included Rathmines.

up to the work.' The tram service to and from Rathmines ran every six minutes. In 1881, three companies amalgamated to form the Dublin United Tramway Company (DUTC) which had 186 trams with more than 1,000 horses. Horse trams lasted until 1901.

Clanging Bells and Crackling Overhead Cables

By then, electrification of the tram routes had been in progress since 1896 and the electric tram provided cheap and efficient service until the late 1940s. The gaily painted green and yellow trams with their garden seats, brass levers, crackling overhead cables and clanging bells became part of Rathmines life. Writing on the DUTC, the National Transport Museum of Ireland explains:

> Trams were especially distinctive, and every one of the four generations of Dublin trams – Open-top, Balcony, Standard and Luxury – was as characteristic of the city as the Custom House or the Halfpenny Bridge. The DUTC management and staff took a special pride in their trams, built at Spa Road Works in Inchicore.

The Tram Dispute and the Dublin Lockout of 1913.

The line through Rathmines was the Terenure line, the number 15, with its terminus at Terenure crossroads. The number 14 route also passed through Rathmines with a terminus and tram shed at Dartry (Diamond Terrace). The old name, Tramway House, is still on the building. The exterior is reminiscent of that bygone tram era. The interior, now in offices, is still open-plan, and one can still imagine the trams trundling in here at the end of their day's journey from Nelson's Pillar to Rathmines.

Just behind Tramway House is a cul-de-sac called Stable Lane. This is a very rural and rustic lane with a very atmospheric old-style house called Ivy Villas and surrounded by towering trees. And nearby, a converted old building is called Holly Mews.

The Vulture of Dartry Hall

Tramway House is only about 100 yards from the former palatial home of William Martin Murphy of Dartry Hall, Orwell Park. The old house itself still retains many of its distinctive and unusual features (e.g. a turret) although adapted to modern usage. He was the founder of the Dublin United Tramway Company (DUTC).

Murphy had lived in the house since around 1883, and his family remained until 1958, so the connection with Dartry Hall was extremely strong. During the 1913 Lockout, the edifice featured in two less-than-flattering cartoons lampooning the man of the house. The *Irish Worker* published 'The Vulture of Dartry Hall' and 'William "Murder" Murphy's Dream of Conquest', leaving the reader in little doubt as to the publication's feelings towards him. He was also a prominent Dublin businessman who owned Clery's Department Store, *The Irish Independent* and the DUTC, as well as the Imperial Hotel. He was director of many railway companies. He served as an MP for a time for Dublin. With his father-in-law, James Lombard, the nationalist MP, he also helped to build many hundreds of houses all over Dublin.

'The Great Appear Great Because We Are on Our Knees'
The Dublin Lockout of 1913 involved employers locking out striking trade union members and the issue of the right to belong to a trade union. The trade union side was led by Jim Larkin of the famous quotation – 'the great appear great because we are on our knees, let us arise'. Murphy was the leader of the employers' side. Murphy, described by Larkin as a 'capitalistic vampire', was chairman of the Dublin Chamber of Commerce, but he was also a staunch Catholic and was actively involved in the St Vincent de Paul Society and various other charities. He was also involved with the nearby Milltown Golf Course.

The tram service continued to decline; the last tram in Dublin city ran on 9 July 1949 and the last in Co. Dublin near Howth Head in 1959. To this day, the Howth Museum celebrates the great era of trams in the city with a number of the original trams on display.

Buses, Poles and Running for Your Life
In time, the No. 15 bus took over the tram route through Rathmines proper. People still recall the early buses, which had a driver, up front in his own little cab, while a conductor stood on the platform at the back and rang the bell for the driver either to stop or move off from the bus stop. There was a long silver hand pole at the edge of the platform for passengers to grab hold of when alighting or disembarking. A frequent sight in Dublin at the time was a late passenger rushing after a moving bus and grabbing hold of the bar just in the nick of time and before the bus gathered speed. The reverse was also a feature, with passengers disembarking as the bus was slowing down. In the process, and in order to maintain balance and slow themselves down, the passenger appeared to be running after the bus he or she had just disembarked from!

6

HIGHWAYS AND BYWAYS

BOUNDARIES, THE DUBLIN PENNY JOURNAL AND FROM COTTAGES TO MANSIONS

There are a number of major roads traversing and delineating Rathmines. The most significant of these is Rathmines Road itself, an ancient route that linked the old medieval city of Dublin with Yewlands (Terenure), Rathfarnham, Tallaght and the Dublin Mountains.

The present-day Rathmines Road was constructed at the turn of the eighteenth century, *c*.1801, and started at Portobello (La

Rathmines Road in the early twentieth century. *Courtesy of William Clegg V*

Touche) Bridge and extended for half a mile to the boundary with Rathgar. Rathgar Road was not constructed for another few decades. In 1833 the *Dublin Penny Journal* reported that Rathmines Road had every type of dwelling including cottages, mansions and villas. The present vista we see from Portobello Bridge towards the Dublin Mountains with the late Georgian/early Victorian-type dwellings on our left has remained virtually unchanged for 200 years.

Grove Road, marking the northern boundary of Rathmines, stretches along the southern banks of the Grand Canal from the bridge to Harold's Cross (Robert Emmet) Bridge. Ontario Terrace and Mountpleasant Avenue mark the Rathmines/Ranelagh boundary. Other roads off the main Rathmines Road include Leinster Road and the Grosvenor environs, Castlewood Avenue and Belgrave Square and from there the Palmerston, Temple and Cowper collection of roads.

THE HALF-MILE ROAD AND THE HIGHWAY TO CULLENSWOOD

Between Rathmines Road Lower and Mount Pleasant Square and linked to the latter, via an archway under No. 31 on the square, is Mountpleasant Avenue. Many of the houses here date from the 1830s onwards. Corrigan's Pub dates from the early twentieth century (1910) and around the corner in the shadow of the impressive green dome of the Church of Our Lady of Refuge is the picturesque curved line of stucco dwellings known as Bessborough Parade dating from the 1840s.

The avenue was an important route in olden times linking Aungier and Camden Streets to Cullenswood and variously called 'the Milltown Path', 'the Highway to Cullenswood' and the 'Half-Mile Road' since this is the distance between the canal at Portobello Bridge and Belgrave Square. From the 1830s onwards, and until the 1860s, house-building continued along this old winding and undulating path, and since it was also the time when the nearby Square was being developed, it assumed the name, Mountpleasant Avenue. Near Gullistan Avenue, building was diverted because the grounds and boundary of the famous Leinster Cricket Club prevented any such works. This club, founded in 1852, moved to Observatory Lane, its present site, in 1865.

SUNDAY EVENINGS WITH GEORGE RUSSELL

One famous resident of this road for a number of years and who lived at No. 28 was George William Russell (1867–1935). He wrote under the pseudonym Æ (signifying the lifelong quest of man), and was a poet, painter, journalist and mystic. He was at the centre of the Irish Literary Revival of the late 1800s and a supporter of nationalist politics. Born in Lurgan, Co. Armagh, in 1867, his family moved to Dublin (Grosvenor Square) in 1878, where he attended Rathmines School. He also attended the Metropolitan School of Art where he formed a lifelong friendship with the future poet William Butler Yeats. He came to mysticism early on and many of his poems reflect this tendency. In 1897, he became Assistant Secretary of the Irish Agricultural Organisation Society (IAOS), started by Horace Plunkett in 1894. As a representative of the IAOS, he travelled extensively throughout Ireland setting up Co-operative Banks. Though his position in the IAOS prohibited him from expressing political opinions, it was no secret that he was a nationalist. During the 1913 Lockout, he wrote an open letter to *The Irish Times* criticising the employers' actions. Russell was also the editor of several newspapers affiliated with the IAOS including The *Irish Homestead* (1905–23) and the leading and very influential literary journal *The Irish Statesmen* (1923–30). Throughout his time with the IAOS he continued to write and publish poetry, essays, plays and novels. He also continued to draw and paint.

1910 – FROM GUINAN'S TO CORRIGAN'S

This pub dates from 1910 and is now also called Corrigan's Mountpleasant Inn. Before that it was called Guinan's and that name is still carved in red stone high up on the front wall. Above it, '1910' is carved into the top gable. The pub achieved a certain fame when a film on the young days of playwright Seán O'Casey, called *Young Cassidy*, was shot in the pub.

GULISTAN'S ARTISANS AND RICHMOND HILL

There is a cluster of nearly hidden avenues containing a virtual hive of artisan dwellings between Mountpleasant Avenue and Rathmines Road and between the Leinster Cricket Club grounds and Richmond Hill. These dwellings were built on the grounds of the original Gulistan House, which consisted of more than three acres of land. The first cottages were built by the Rathmines and Rathgar Urban District Council in the decades before and after the turn of the nineteenth century.

THE SWAN, THE STRUMPET AND THE FEIS CEOIL

Nearly 100 years before, in the early years of the nineteenth century, work had begun on the bigger, three-storey houses on Richmond Hill that stretched to Rathmines Road and opposite St Mary's College. An archway underneath No. 31 Mount Pleasant Square links the fine curved square with the new road and beyond. The new road was built along what was a path along part of the River Swan, which wound its way towards Ranelagh. House-building was complete by *c.*1837.

The writer and poet Dora Sigerson Shorter and her family lived at No. 17 in the 1860s and '70s. Her father was the renowned man of letters, one of the founders of Feis Ceoil, surgeon and Professor of Zoology, George Sigerson. His highly regarded book, *Bards of the Gael and Gall*, was published in 1897. The Bernadette Players drama group used to meet in the old red-bricked building across the road. A new apartment block near the site, called Bernadette Hall, is a reminder of the former hall where the drama group met. No. 12 was the former home of the best-selling romance novelist, Annie M.P. Smithson, where she died in 1948. James Plunkett, author of the famous book *Strumpet City*, lived in No. 25.

RENOWNED ARCHITECTS AND BESSBOROUGH PARADE

Around the corner from Corrigan's Pub, just off Mountpleasant Avenue, is Bessborough Parade, a quiet residential curved road dating from the 1840s. Although a cul-de-sac, there is a hidden zig-zag passage from it to the front of Rathmines Church. The big copper dome dominates the pleasant vista – it's visible from all over Rathmines, and here, close up, it's just huge and inescapable. On one side of the street, there's a row of terraced houses, fancy fanlights and ornate external plasterwork pieces, and with small front gardens. On the other side, though, the architecture is from the late twentieth century – the Hall House by the renowned Grafton Architects, and a house beside it, by similarly renowned architects De Blacam and Meagher.

MORRIS MINORS – STRIVING FOR PERFECTION

Richmond Hill brings us back to Rathmines Road Lower. At each side of the striking building that is Grand Canal House there is an arched and ornate gateway leading in or out of the former G.A. Brittain Motor Factory. One in particular is still in situ as it was when it was a factory, with the word 'IN' still emblazoned on the arched glass above the entrance. In a very interesting article for *Architecture Ireland*, Cormac Murray explains that in here, and along Grove Road, 'passers-by could once observe the steel carcasses of Morris Minors on the assembly line'. At the 1948 motor show in Earls Court, London, the Morris Minor was heralded as 'the world's supreme small car' and the manufacturers even said that it 'approached perfection'! The factory in Rathmines stayed in production from the late

1940s until 1975. For decades, the Morris Minor was one of the best-selling cars in Ireland. Part of the site was later taken over by Taylors Neon Signs (located next-door) and the remainder subsequently was demolished for houses and apartments. These are called Portobello Harbour and Cois Eala (beside the swans).

SIGNAGE AND LANDMARKS - WHY GO BALD AND BONO

The Morris Minor works on Grove Road were eventually taken over by a completely different enterprise – Taylor's Signs, a company that specialised in colourful neon signs and lights. Taylor's doesn't just produce signs – it produces landmarks. The Hafner's Sausages sign on O'Connell Street was one example of their eye-catching work. Another one on South Great George's Street, named 'Why go Bald?', soon became equally famous. It is an advertisement for the Universal Hair and Scalp Clinic (the longest running of its kind in Ireland), which21387498273648 is situated right behind it. This flashing sign using red and yellow colours is of a young man, alternately without hair and frowning, then with hair and smiling. It has survived for over seventy years on the same site and has been the subject of much discussion, amusement and at times admiration over the years. One such fan is U2's Bono. It has also appeared on the silver screen. Eagle-eyed viewers of *Educating Rita* or *A Man of No Importance* will spot the vintage neon sign in the background.

NOT LABOURING IN VAIN AT THE YMCA

Between Portobello Bridge and the junction with Grove Park there are two distinctive buildings – Grand Canal House and the YMCA. The former has nice garlanded urns atop the front elevation and nicely placed between the chimneys. At each side of the attractive building are the former entrance and exit doors, with arced glass windows over them, of Brittain Motors. Further along is the 1911 red-bricked YMCA building, now part of the Leeson School of Music. Carved above the original entrance are the immortal words: 'Except the Lord build the house – they labour in vain that build it.'

QUIRKY AND DRAMATIC – FROM HENRY GRATTAN TO QUEEN ANNE

Near the junction of Grove Park (No. 107) and Rathmines Road Lower is the very striking detached red-bricked Kensington Lodge house, full of character and architectural interest with highly decorative flourishes both inside (including intricate stucco work in the living room) and outside.

The house is the work of prolific British architect William Isaac Chambers who designed it for himself in 1822. Built in the Queen Anne style, it is replete with a fine curved gable, star- and spoked-wheel windows, several elaborately coloured windows, two carved ladies wearing diadems at the upper level, and floral patterns and bands over windows. The house was lauded by *The Irish Builder*, who were particularly taken with the use of terracotta mouldings – quite the Dublin trailblazer in that regard:

> We have inspected some specimens of this terra cotta and more artistic or beautifully modelled work it is difficult to conceive; every outline is as sharp and well relieved as if straight from a carver's chisel; the colour is very good; and we are sure that, when once introduced into this country, it will meet with the approval and demand it certainly deserves.

Grove Park and Grove Road (which stretches from Portobello Bridge to Harold's Cross Bridge, overlooking the Grand Canal) derived its name from Grove House, a house situated in the area and with links to Henry Grattan and his family. Apparently, it had been granted to Grattan by the citizens of Dublin after the achievement of legislative independence for Ireland in 1782. Grattan's Parliament met in the present-day Bank of Ireland building (called the Irish Houses of Parliament) on College Green.

ART DECO, THE KODAK BUILDING AND LISSENFIELD HOUSE

Further along the main road is the distinctive and bulky white-painted Kodak House building on the corner with Blackberry Lane. Kodak House is one of two listed Art Deco buildings in Rathmines. It was designed by Donnelly, Moore and Keatinge, completed in 1930, with later modifications by William Sedgewick Keatinge (1949–51). In recent years, a complete refurbishment was undertaken to convert the building into modern office space by Paul Keogh Architects.

The apartment complex, Lissenfield, was once the site of Lissenfield House, the home of the Mulcahy family until the 1980s. General Richard Mulcahy was active in the War of Independence. His son was the renowned heart specialist Professor Richard Mulcahy. The old house is gone yet the original winding driveway remains intact and the new development is surrounded by a number of lingering old trees. Beside Lissenfield is a Woman's Refuge which opened in 1985. It was the first purpose-built project of its kind in Ireland.

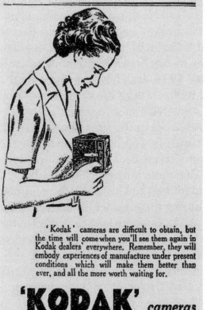

'Kodak' cameras are difficult to obtain, but the time will come when you'll see them again in Kodak dealers' everywhere. Remember, they will embody experiences of manufacture under present conditions which will make them better than ever, and all the more worth waiting for.

'KODAK' *cameras*

KODAK LIMITED, KODAK HOUSE, RATHMINES, DUBLIN.

Early advertisement for Kodak Cameras.

ST MARY'S AND THE KELSO LAUNDRY

Next door is St Mary's College, dating from *c*.1890, with Cathal Brugha Barracks behind dating from between 1810 and 1815.The green-domed Catholic church across the road dates from *c*.1856.

Near the Military Road leading into the barracks was the former Princess Cinema and nearby, the Kelso Laundry. The only reminder of the latter is the original red-bricked facade now fronting an apartment complex. It was established by businesswoman Jean Kelso in 1914 and survived until 1994.

FIVE GENERATIONS OF SHOE REPAIR – WILLIAM CLEGG V

Between Richmond Hill and Observatory Lane there is a variety of shops and businesses, including the Orange Tree bakery, Domino's Pizzas, the sombre and black-painted Blackbird Pub, a chemist shop and of course the renowned Clegg's Shoe Repair shop. This latter is a veritable landmark, not only in Rathmines, but also in the wider Dublin, having been in continuous business with the same family since 1934. It is now managed by the affable and always helpful William Clegg V, a veritable walking encyclopaedia on all things involving shoe repairs.

In an interview with Rose Doyle of the *Irish Times* in 2012, William gave his family's history and his knowledge of the business shone forth. His enthusiasm, dedication and love of the business are inspiring, and one could only conclude that being a master cobbler is a vocation for him and his family. Not for him little elves working away during the night while he slept in the overhead loft. In the interview he recounted the early days of the business, including the heel bar in Roche's Stores where customers availed of the repaired 'While U Wait' quick service. He even differentiated between the quality and style of men's and women's shoes and the requirements needed to design and care for each.

Yak Traks, Horse Hair Brushes and Saddle Soap
It is worthwhile just to pop into the shop on Lower Rathmines Road to view the range of items he sells and services he provides

– all designed to look after shoes, belts, handbags, coats – leather in whatever form it takes, and to ensure comfort and lasting quality to repairs undertaken. Here you will find yak trak ice grips, sprays, foams, creams, wet blockers, horse-hair brushes and saddle soap. There was a time also when one would see, on a Saturday evening, queues of people waiting outside Clegg's for their shoe repairs so they would be well shod for Sunday Mass. An interesting old street sign outside the shop advertises 'Black and Tan' shoe polish and hails from an era when 'the quality' lived in Rathmines and army officers, based in Portobello Barracks, also lived in areas such as nearby Grosvenor Square.

Teas and Keys – A Film Star of Real Character

Another side to William Clegg V is that he is a film star in his own right, having appeared in the Barry's Tea marketing campaign (which included huge billboards everywhere) and in Fr Peter McVerry's Keys4Homes ad campaign. In the former advert he poses in his shop, surrounded by shelves of shoes, holding a mug of tea and with the words 'not too strong' and 'teas of real character' at the bottom of the image. The second ad was designed to raise awareness and much needed funds for the homeless and features William at the start of the video cutting keys in his shop.

OBSERVATORY LANE – TELESCOPES, PERISCOPES AND PRINTING BANKNOTES

An 1837 map of the Rathmines shows an 'Observatory' not too far from the Grand Canal – near Charlemont Bridge. In the early nineteenth century, the maker of scientific and astronomy instruments, Thomas Grubb (1800–78), lived at No.1 Ranelagh Road and had his workshop nearby – hence 'Observatory' on the map. Grubb was a billiard table maker, a clock maker, and then an optician who diversified into making intricate scientific instruments including telescopes and lenses. In the 1830s, he had set up an engineering works called Optical and Mechanical Works, and built himself a small observatory on the site. Grubb also constructed precision instruments for Trinity College Dublin. In the early 1840s, he became

Melbourne Telescope in Grubb's Factory in Rathmines.

'Engineer of the Bank of Ireland' on College Green, where he was responsible for designing, constructing and maintaining the machinery used in the production of banknotes.

Birr Castle and the Melbourne Mirror

On the occasion of receiving a commission to build a new 48-inch reflector for Melbourne Observatory, Grubb established a new works just off the Rathmines Road, on what is now known as Observatory Lane. Working with his son Howard, Grubb's company thrived and throughout his career he built some of the world's greatest telescopes, many of which are still in operation. Amongst his many achievements is the world-famous telescope in Birr Castle, Co. Offaly, which he helped to build. His telescopes are still used in Dunsink, Armagh, Greenwich observatories and elsewhere. During the First World War, the Grubb Works provided most of the periscopes for the Royal Navy's submarines. Grubb was elected a Member of the Royal Irish Academy in 1839 and a Fellow of the Royal Society in 1864.

The Great Melbourne Telescope, built by Thomas Grubb in 1868. Erected at the Melbourne Observatory in 1869, it was, at the time of its unveiling, the second largest in the world and was ground-breaking it is design.
Courtesy of HXHS

HOME TO EMINENT JOURNALIST, SOLICITOR AND STATESMAN

Today, the only reminder of the former Rathmines Fire Station (opposite the Library) are the distinctive old, large red folding doorways. This was operational from the late nineteenth century until the 1980s. The local historian Eamon MacThomáis was born in a cottage behind the station, his father being the Captain of the Fire Station. The Fire Station is no longer used but the original red doors to the front and the insides are much as before. A laneway separating the station from the Town Hall once led to a group of houses called Holmeville. It was here that Charles Gavan Duffy, Young Irelander, co-founder of *The Nation* and later eminent Prime Minister of Victoria in Australia, lived for a time in No. 5 in 1844. Today, a narrow and little-known footpath links Rathmines Road to Gulistan Cottages.

WORLD CHAMPIONS AND PIZZA HURLING

Just beyond the Town Hall is the famous Manifesto Restaurant, apparently the dream of two good friends, and twice winner of gold medals in the World Pizza Championships. One of the prize-winning pizzas was called 'Mamy' (Al Jolson sang: 'I'd walk a million miles for one of your pizzas, Mamy'). Not surprising, since the first item you see on walking through the doors is a giant wood-fired pizza oven. Chef-owner Lucio Paduano hails from the Campania region in the south of Italy and his passion for creative and high-quality food is reflected in the menus. Food critic Paulo Tullio visited Manifesto and his views included words such as 'sensational', 'perfectly cooked', 'genuinely Italian meal' and 'beautifully combined flavours'. Even the wines had pedigrees traced back to Roman times, he noted. Furthermore, during the meal, the lights were dimmed and the chef put on 'a remarkable display of pizza hurling and twirling'. According to Ernie Whalley, another food critic, 'It's not just the Michelin-starred places that can provide the all-round perfect dining experience' after a meal in Manifesto. He awarded the restaurant five stars!

ECHOES OF QUAKERISM AND THE CAMPAIGN FOR FEMALE SUFFRAGE

In their later years, famous Irish Quakers Anna and Thomas Haslam had a shop along where the Swan Centre is located on Rathmines Road. They lived nearby at No. 125 Leinster Road. Interestingly, the fine and distinctive detached house on this tree-lined road is located in its own grounds, yet is not a listed property – but the entrance bollards, spud-stones, gates and railings are!

Both lifelong Quakers, Anna and Thomas Halsam were married in 1854 and were staunch campaigners for social reform from the late nineteenth century onwards. As Carmel Quinlan explains in her 2005 book, *Genteel Revolutionaries:*

Anna and Thomas Haslam and the Irish Women's Movement ... were central to the progression of the nascent feminist agenda in the early decades of the twentieth century. The couple founded the Dublin Women's Suffrage Association in 1876 and campaigned for the repeal of the Contagious Diseases Act in the same decade, a campaign that outraged polite society, dealing as it did with issues like prostitution and venereal diseases. But the Halsams refused to shy away from difficult issues. Thomas wrote extensively on topics such as birth control, and Anna was influential in the crusade for education and votes for women.

From Suffrage to Flowers and Flags – Winning the Vote
In her later years, Anna ran a stationery and toy business on Rathmines Road to help support herself and her ailing husband. Her resolve remained strong, however. Quinlan, this time writing in the *Irish Times* in 2012, paints a picture of a 90-year-old Anna Halsam:

In 1918, a woman of almost ninety, she went to the polls surrounded by flowers and flags, flanked by unionist, Irish Party and Sinn Féin women, united in her honour to celebrate the victory of the vote. This display of unity by activist women from all shades of political opinion acknowledged Anna's pivotal role in the fight for the vote.

Anna died in 1922, the same year that the Irish Free State extended the vote to all men and women over the age of 21.

LEINSTER ROAD AND THE RIFF-RAFF

Facing the Town Hall (1896) is the gradually sloping Leinster Road (1840) that links Rathmines to Harold's Cross Road. At one time, there were iron gates at each end of the road to ease the flow of disreputable types into the area. In the large houses, with many having steps leading up to the entrances, lived many famous individuals. Countess Markievicz and her husband

Casimir lived in No. 49b. Lord and Lady Longford lived across the road in a detached mansion called Grosvenor Park. No. 40 was the home of the old Fenian John O'Leary. Thomas and Anna Haslam lived in No. 125.

PRINCE ARTHUR AND THE FOUR PROVINCES

Returning to Rathmines Road, across from the Swan Centre entrance, is Leinster Square. The architecture of some of the late Georgian and early Victorian houses on Leinster Square and Prince Arthur Terrace is a joy to behold. It is more of a road than a square – rather, two short roads in a T-shape – and the earlier, elegant houses were built between 1830 and 1843. No. 7 was added in 1852 and No. 1 around 1877. These fine houses were designed mainly by John de Courcy Butler. Butler's entry in the *Dictionary of Irish Architects*, 1720–1940, elaborates:

> Butler and his neighbour Arthur Williamson ... leased adjoining pieces of land near the south corner of Rathmines Road and the future Leinster Road. Between 1830 and 1837, they built six houses each on their plots to form Leinster Terrace.

Eventually, they decided to call the combined terraces Leinster Square, although strictly speaking, it is not quite a square. Later in the 1850's, the western end of the square was developed and extended to form Prince Arthur Terrace. There is a quaint and winding back lane with steps, leading from here to Summerville Place and the Rathmines Road.

A ROLL CALL OF NOTABLES

Both Leinster Square and Prince Arthur Terrace have houses that were childhood homes of the writer Patrick Lafcadio Hearn (No. 30 Leinster Square and No. 3 Prince Arthur Terrace). Other notables that lived on the square included the Fenian James

Stephens, who lived in No. 2 in 1914. Charles Gavan Duffy lived in No. 4 in the 1840s. Houston Collison who collaborated with Percy French lived at No. 6. Leinster Square. It was home to Thomas Grubb and Sir Howard Grubb (Nos. 21 and 23), James Stephens (No. 2) and Charles Gavin Duffy for a short time at No. 4. The square was also gated for many years, a tiny reminder of which still lingers on two bollards on the Rathmines Road boundary.

MURDER AFOOT AND MAMIE CADDEN

Around the corner from Leinster Square and facing the Swan Centre is No. 183 Rathmines Road. This had an interesting former occupant and one who achieved great notoriety in the conservative Ireland of the 1940s and 1950s. Mary Anne Cadden (1891–1959) was a midwife known to her patients as 'Mamie'. She had purchased the property in 1931 and for years operated her own private maternity nursing home. This would have catered for the well-to-do in the area and beyond. It was called St Maelruain's, a name giving it added respectability at a time when such an attribute was de rigueur for so many aspects of a class-conscious society.

From St Maelruain's to Mountjoy – The Nurse Falls Foul
Besides delivering and caring for babies and their mothers, Nurse Cadden provided the outsourcing of fostering services for unwanted babies at an added fee. Foster families received a fee for caring for the child. Over time she added abortion and contraception to her services and this was at a time in Ireland when the provision of such services was strictly illegal. It was said that her services were an open secret in 1930s Dublin. Alas, however, she was forced to close her lucrative business in 1939 after a newborn infant was found abandoned on the side of a road in County Meath. Subsequent Garda investigations led them to Rathmines. Nurse Cadden was sentenced to a year's hard labour in Mountjoy Prison.

Notorious Murder Trial of Mamie Cadden

Following her release from prison, Nurse Cadden returned to providing illegal maternity services, not in Rathmines but at various Dublin addresses including Hume Street. Unfortunately for her, because of her conviction and prison record the professional body for midwives had her struck off. So, in a way, her destiny was marked out for her. She was convicted again in 1945 after one of her clients developed complications after a botched abortion, needed urgent hospitalisation and pointed the finger of blame at Cadden. She was sentenced to five years in prison. Not deterred on her release, she resumed her old trade from Hume Street. Unfortunately one of her patients, Helen O'Reilly, died while having an abortion. Cadden dumped her body on the pavement outside her clinic and quickly the Gardaí knew who the culprit was. This time she was tried for murder, a trial which attracted enormous attention for many reasons, but in particular because of her notoriety. She found guilty and sentence to be hanged in 1956. This was later commuted to life imprisonment and she was sent to Dundrum Criminal Lunatic Asylum. She died there in 1959.

ONE OF DUBLIN'S FIRST CINEMAS

Moving past the Swan Centre brings us to the junction of Castlewood Avenue and Upper Rathmines Road. The former Stella Cinema faces the junction. This cinema was designed by Higginbotham & Stafford and built in 1923. One of the earliest cinemas in the city, and the largest cinema in Dublin at the time of its construction, the Stella Theatre is an architectural delight with impressive original features such as the façade, the ceilings, the mosaic floors and the decorative stair balustrades. In addition to its architectural merits, it is a socially and culturally significant building, an exemplar of the many cinemas and dance halls to emerge in the 1920s and 1930s, reflecting the burgeoning popularity of film and dance culture.

THE BELFAST BANK AND THE BANK OF IRELAND – ARCHITECTURAL SET PIECES

Around the corner from the Stella is the site of the red-bricked former Belfast Bank (1901) with its distinctive turret. Designed by the Belfast-based architect Vincent Craig (brother of the first NI Prime Minister, Lord Craigavon), it still bears the coat of arms and motto of Belfast, on a terracotta plaque set into the wall. The motto reads, 'pro tanto quid retribuamus', meaning 'what shall we give in return for so much'. Located at the junction with Wynnefield Road, it is quite a large building, a picturesque Scottish Baronial copy, complete with a corner turret.

The building is not the only impressive bank building on Rathmines Road. Facing the Swan Centre is the Bank of Ireland's stand-alone classic brownstone/red-brick premises. Located at 175 Lower Rathmines Road, it has splendid external architecture, ornate plasterwork and eye-catching timber work within the banking hall. There is also an old clock that has to be hand-wound every so often. The building is a protected structure.

Advertisement for the 'imposing' Lees department store opposite the Stella. The date '1910' is still visible today.

ABNER BROWNS: HIPPIES USE THE BACKDOOR!

Where else can you get a haircut and see a live band in the same place? In Rathmines, of course! Right beside the former bank is another landmark – this time a barbershop which has been in business for over twenty years. But this is not just any barbershop. It is Abner Brown's, where a notice in the window beside the entrance strongly advises: 'Hippies Use the Backdoor. No Exceptions!' An arrow points one in the direction. So, even before you enter, you know you are in for an experience. The inside looks like a rock 'n' roll experience museum with two turntables and DJ's desktop. The walls are plastered with album covers and all sorts of paraphernalia about twentieth-century music – and not just the rock 'n' roll variety. Gramophones and music instruments are scattered about as if waiting for their owners to pop in and strike up a beat. And that is exactly what happens! This barbershop is also a favourite haunt for passing musicians who call in and perform live while the barbers give their customers their haircut. Mostly, however, the sessions are in the evenings, just in case a barber was distracted and accidentally cuts your ear off! If so, you could pop into the nearby and legendary Martin Slattery's Pub for a pint and drown your sorrows.

Top Chop Shop for Your Mop

All in all, it is an intimate music venue at its best and bands like Ash, the Hot Sprockets, Mongoose, Sive and Molly Sterling, Duke Special and many more have played. Sessions at Abner Brown's set a new bar for barbers. As one customer noted: 'this is a top chop shop for your mop. Everything was amazing. The vibes, the people, the music.' David Judge is the man who owns the venue and is the one behind the hugely successful Rathmines 'Canalaphonic' Music Festival for Portobello and Rathmines.

LENEHAN'S THE COLOSSUS

A few doors around the corner, at 7–9 Rathgar Road, was the home for many years of Lenehan's Hardware Store, famous for hardware since 1865, and which finally closed its doors in 2015. The owner's retirement prompted the closure. According to a customer prior to its closing:

> This is one of those businesses that you won't even realise exists until you absolutely desperately need it. It seems like there are not many small hardware stores still in business, and they've all been replaced by big-box retailers in suburban industrial parks. Lenehan's remains, bestriding Rathmines like a colossus. As colossal as a small hardware shop can be anyway … A quirky little hardware store, they're offering a service that's becoming harder to find by the day.

KING OF KEBABS – FROM ABRACADABRA TO ABRAKEBABRA

The year 1982 was an important one in Ireland's – and Rathmines' – culinary history, for it was in that year that the country experienced a doner kebab mania when Abrakebabra opened up in Rathmines, offering this new food for Irish palates. A kebab is a Turkish dish, usually featuring lamb or pork cooked on a vertical rotisserie, skewer or spit. The meat is then sliced vertically into thin shavings and served in a pitta with salad and sauces. Abrakebabra was to the forefront of this new culinary experience and today still sells the Original Doner – spit roasted lamb with slaw, tomato, chilli and herb garlic sauces as well as many other variations including chicken and spicy beef kebabs.

FROM HO HO TO THE P.O.

On the opposite side of Rathmines Road, facing the Ho Ho Chinese takeaway and adjacent supermarket (which has had many names over the years), is the grey-fronted Art Deco-style Post Office (1934). This was designed by Howard Cooke of the Office of Public Works. The doorway surround is particularly interesting, as is the interior with its original counters and flooring.

BOXTY, CODDLE AND THE BRETZEL BAKERY

Until quite recently, there was an old family business beside the Post Office called the Bretzel Bakery. This was a branch of the main business which is still located on Lennox Street in nearby Portobello, and has been for generations. Luckily, the residents of Rathmines may still enjoy the comforting aromas wafting towards them over Portobello Bridge. The Bretzel is a modern-day bakery steeped in tradition and history since 1870. The Bretzel Bakery makes the case that it is 'as much a part of Dublin culinary history as Boxty or a bowl of Coddle' – and it is certainly as popular. They pride themselves on their heritage, boasting that they have used the same recipe for challah (Jewish festival sesame bread) since the bakery opened in the nineteenth century. Some of its signature breads (many with German, Italian and French influences) include sourdough, granary loaf, country store (which contains flax seeds and sunflower seeds), tortano crown (potato bread using Rooster potatoes and honey), stoneground and Pain de Campagne (French-style rustic bread).

The Natural Bakery, across from Slattery's Pub, a relatively new enterprise, also offers freshly baked artisan breads every day. Recently, it started a Grain Project, 'to include even more Irish ingredients and developing flour from 100% Irish wheat and cereals'.

TRANQUILA CONVENT AND HOLLYFIELD BUILDINGS

Continuing past another few long-established family businesses, including Gallagher's TV, Deveney's and the Uppercross House Hotel, we then notice old terraces of three- and four-storey mid-Victorian houses with their upper floor windows embraced with decorative box railing. These include Carlton and Summerville terraces. At the junction, we have Church Avenue with the Church of the Holy Trinity (1828) and the fine surrounding houses built from the 1840s onwards. Across the main road, the red-bricked one-storey building is the former Church of Ireland national school, now the home of the Rathmines and Rathgar Musical Society (1913).

The site of the former Rathmines Castle (1816–20) is now occupied by the Kildare Place School, Alexandra School and the Church of Ireland Training College. Next door is the Tranquila Lodge, a reminder of the Tranquila Convent of the Carmelite nuns who moved from here in the 1970s. The site is now Tranquila Park containing a children's playground. Across the road is a new development of houses in Rathmines Close, site of the former Hollyfield Buildings that were built on the site of what was Hollyfield House. Hollyfield Buildings was the birthplace of Martin Cahill, known as 'The General'.

DREAMING OF CRUMBLES, CREAM BOMBES, CARAMEL AND CHOCOLATE – QUEUEING AT LAWLOR'S

Along here there are a number of well-established and popular shops and businesses, including Lawlor's Butchers, where you are guaranteed a place in the queue on Christmas morning. However, if any attempt is made to skip the queue you will invariably end up like the forlorn sheep dangling over the entrance. Next door is the renowned Fothergill's bakery and delicatessen, managed by the very capable and friendly Tom O'Connor. Here you will be spoilt with tarts, crumbles, Bailey's Irish Cream bombes, cheesecakes and many more mouthwatering and most appetising cakes and pastries, including the shortbread covered with caramel and topped with chocolate. You might prefer the Viennese Fingers or the Victoria Sponge. Not to mention the Gateau Dianne! The cheese counter offers myriad tasty options, and the shelves are stuffed with pesto, vinaigrettes, chutneys and exotic coffees.

THE ROLLING-SKATING RINK – AN IDEAL PLACE TO SETTLE DOWN

Rathmines Park, a narrow avenue tucked away off the main road, is the location of a number of businesses and leads to a hidden and quaint enclave of Victorian one- and two-storey red-bricked houses with bay windows. The circle of houses faces onto a green area. The area was once the site of a roller-skating rink in the late nineteenth century.

Dartry Road once began at No. 215 Upper Rathmines Road, where there is a plaque on the front elevation of the house that reads: 'Fitzwilliam Terrace, Lr Dartry Road, Upr Rathmines, 1905'.

On the opposite side of the road, we have the turns for Fortfield Terrace and Cowper Road. One striking residence stands out along here – Fortfield House, at the corner of Cowper Road and Fortfield Gardens – probably the oldest house in the area, dating from 1740. In the early 1900s this area was considered to be on the outskirts of Dublin, and was described in the *Irish Times* as 'an ideal place to settle down'.

7

THE BELGRAVE–
PALMERSTON ENCLAVE

DOGS AND HORSES AND
THE JOYCE FAMILY

To the east of Rathmines and Highfield roads is the Palmerston-Temple-Cowper area that stretches north to Castlewood Avenue.

Most of the houses and villas on Castlewood Avenue date from the 1850s. William Osborne RHA and his family lived in No. 5 from 1855 until his death in 1901. He devoted himself to painting animals, mainly dogs and horses. His son, Walter Osborne, was an even more renowned artist and remains one of Ireland's most eminent artists to this day. No. 23 was the home of James Joyce for a number of years. Three of his siblings were born there – Margaret, Stanislaus and Charles. He was born at Brighton Square.

A SHORT BACK AND SIDES OR A
CLOSE SHAVE WITH A TRAM

Since 1912, No. 38 Castlewood Avenue has been the home of the renowned Doran's Barbers, one of the oldest surviving barbershops in Dublin. (The Waldorf on Westmoreland Street has been trading since 1929 and is another veritable institution.) Jimmy and Willie Doran were born, raised and worked here for decades until well into the twenty-first century and this institution has long been part of the life of Rathmines. The ownership changed hands in recent years but has retained the original name and appearance, both inside and outside. Here you will see the same polished wooden floor, benches along the walls, two washbasins, postcards from all over the world, and much historical memorabilia.

On Thursday, 20 April 1916, Padraig and Willie Pearse went into Doran's for their last haircut before their surrender and subsequent excecutions. John Doran, father of Jimmy and Willie Doran, remembered the event. 'They did not speak much, as they awaited their turn in the chair. But then they never did.' The young John had no foreboding that he was giving the brothers their last haircut.

Jimmy Doran, born in 1916, remembers the No.18 tram, with its red triangle identifier, passing the front door of the shop. Jimmy worked in the shop for nearly 70 years, only retiring in 1998.

A HANDSOME ARRAY OF HOUSES

Prior to the 1830s, what is now Belgrave Square was a field bisected by the Swan River; there was also a path, later to become Belgrave Road and then Belgrave Square East.

The development of the square dates largely from the 1860s. The main developer was John Holmes, who lived in the vicinity, at Castlewood House. The fields in the area had been taken over by the Rathmines Town Commissioners in late 1851 and Belgrave Avenue (on the south of the present square) was the first terrace built. The park was made public in the 1970s.

The architectural historian Maurice Craig described the east side of the square as 'a handsome array of semi-detached houses'. The sculptor Joseph Watkins RHA (1838–1971) lived at No.49 and one of his models was Charles Dickens. At 59 Belgrave Square North there is a barely visible plaque embedded into the wall with 'Kensinton (sic) Terrace' on it.

PROPERTY, POLITICS AND DYNASTIES

Beyond Belgrave Square, and at the junction with Palmerston Road, is Belgrave Road. Some of the houses (Nos. 6–13) were built by the developer Patrick Plunkett, father of Count Plunkett and grandfather of the 1916 leader Joseph Mary Plunkett. Plunkett senior (who lived in one of the Belgrave Road houses) built many of the houses in the vicinity, including at Palmerton Road, Cowper Road, Windsor Road, Ormond Road and Palmerston Park. He used Edward Carson (father of Sir Edward) as his architect. His son, Count George Plunkett, became involved in politics before and after the 1916 Rising. Interestingly, Michael Collins worked for the Plunketts, collecting rents from their many properties. Many of the tenants were from the affluent middle classes, in particular military personnel and senior civil servants.

A HOTBED OF FEMINISM AND NATIONALISM

Belgrave Road was also home to Dr Kathleen Lynn (No. 9) one of the co-founders (with Madeleine Ffrench-Mullen) of St Ultan's Children's Hospital in 1918. A staunch nationalist and feminist, and a member of the Irish Citizen Army, she participated in the 1916 Rising as a medical officer. Fearghal McGarry, writing in *History Ireland* (Vol. 21, 2013), states that Dr Lynn also attributed her politicisation 'to the influence of [Helena] Molony [a prominent republican, socialist and feminist who fought in the 1916 Rising], who had stayed at her Belgrave Road home following an illness: "We used to have long talks and she converted me to the national movement. She was a very clever and attractive girl with a tremendous power of making friends."'

Lynn House, the headquarters of the Irish Medical Council, on Rathmines Road, near Portobello Bridge, is named after her.

FROM ICA AND RUDC TO BCG

For many years (1915–44), Dr Lynn shared her house with another woman – Madeleine Ffrench-Mullen (1880–1944), a revolutionary and labour activist and who also took part in the 1916 Rising. Ffrench-Mullen was a member of the radical nationalist women's organisation Inghinidhe na hÉireann and she was also in the Irish Citizens Army. She was arrested and imprisoned after the Rising and later joined Sinn Féin and was elected for Rathmines District Council in 1920. Years later, Lynn and Ffrench-Mullen established a vaccination project for impoverished children. There is little doubt that, without this undertaking, thousands of children would have succumbed to TB, and this eventually led to the foundation of the BCG programme, which has vaccinated all babies since the 1950s. Dr Lynn died in 1955.

HANNA SHEEHY, NORA CONNOLLY AND UNA BRENNAN

In No. 7 lived Hanna Sheehy. She was co-founder of the Irishwomen's Franchise League. There is a plaque on the exterior wall of the College of Music (on Rathmines Road) to commemorate her teaching in that building when it was the Rathmines Technical Institute (later the College of Commerce). She married Francis Skeffington and they changed their surnames to Sheehy-Skeffington.

In that same college, another 1916 activist worked years later – Nora Connolly-O'Brien, a daughter of the executed leader, James Connolly. After she got married to Seamus O'Brien in 1922 they rented a flat on Belgrave Road for a number of years. Robert and Una Brennan, also active in 1916, and he later with Sinn Féin, lived in No.10.

A postcard of Wexford's Easter Rising leaders Séamus Rafter, Robert Brennan and Seán Etchingham. *Picture: National Library of Ireland 1916, Bob Brennan*

THE IRISH VOLUNTEER AND THE DOLPHIN

Other important figures that lived in the vicinity of the Holy Trinity Church included Desmond Broe (No. 8 Belgrave Road) the well-known sculptor with monumental works on Harold's Cross Road/St Clare's Avenue. Much of Broe's time was taken up with ecclesiastical work for Dublin churches, along with many IRA memorials. Perhaps his most famous work is the Irish Volunteer in Phibsboro. John Joseph O'Callaghan, the late nineteenth-century architect of many buildings and churches in Dublin including St Mary's Church on Haddington Road and the famous Dolphin Hotel on Essex Street in Dublin's Temple Bar, lived on Cambridge Road, nearby.

A ROLL CALL OF POLITICAL
ROYALTY – PALMERSTON ROAD

Palmerston Road, a long tree-lined road, containing grand three-storey houses, links Belgrave Square/Road to Palmerston Park. It was named after Henry John Temple, 3rd Viscount Palmerston, a British Prime Minister who died in 1865. It was Patrick Plunkett, grandfather of 1916 leader Joseph Mary Plunkett, who had started building houses here in the 1850s. It took approximately ten years to complete the building.

Fittingly, a number of Irish Taoisigh and prominent politicians lived on this road, including Seán Lemass, Garret Fitzgerald, Alfie Byrne and Desmond O'Malley (former Fianna Fáil government minister and founder of the Progressive Democrats political party). The wider constituency also had a number of significant political representatives including former Taoiseach, John A. Costello. It was he who declared Ireland a Republic in 1949, led Ireland's first coalition government, and faced into the Mother and Child Crisis of the early 1950s. Another long-time TD for this constituency (now called Dublin Bay South) was the man who heralded in that crisis – Dr Noel Browne. A government minister, Seán MacEntee, also represented the area for many years. Other names not forgotten include Seán Moore, John Gormley, Lucinda Creighton, Ruairí Quinn, Eoin Ryan, Frances Fitzgerald, Richie Ryan, Gerard Brady and Michael McDowell. Interestingly, the constituency (created as Dublin South East in 1947 and changed to Dublin Bay South at the 2016 general election) was, geographically, the smallest in the country, and with a diverse socio-economic profile.

'IS MISE LE MEAS' AND
GARRET THE GOOD

The Twelve Apostles and the Cairo Gang
Seán Francis Lemass (1899–1971) was one of the most prominent Irish politicians of the twentieth century, a Taoiseach in the 1960s and one that liked to sign his letters with 'is mise

le meas' (literally 'myself with respect' or in common parlance, 'yours sincerely') which rhymed with his surname.

Lemass, who lived at No. 53 Palmerston Road, served as Taoiseach from 1959 until 1966. He was a veteran of the Easter Rising (he was just 17 at the time), after which he remained an active member of the Irish Volunteers. In his 1970 book, *The IRA*, Tim Pat Coogan identifies Lemass as one of the so-called 'Apostles' that were involved in the killing of British agents during the notorious events of Bloody Sunday, in which the undercover 'Cairo Gang' was obliterated. In revenge, the Black and Tans killed fourteen innocent civilians at a football match in Croke Park. Lemass was arrested in December 1920 and interned at Ballykinlar Camp, County Down.

Founding Member of Fianna Fáil

With his background in the Irish Volunteers, and his commitment and activities during the long struggle for Irish independence, Lemass was a popular candidate for the Dáil. He ran successfully for Sinn Féin in a Dublin South by-election in November 1924 and he was returned consistently as TD until the constituency was abolished in 1948 (he then ran for Dublin South-Central with continuing success until he retired in 1969). A founding member of Fianna Fáil (established in 1926), he held various positions in government, including several years as Tánaiste.

The Changing of the Guard

On 23 June 1959, Lemass succeeded Éamon de Valera as leader of Fianna Fáil and Taoiseach. De Valera was a tough act to follow, but Lemass quickly established himself and brought a more youthful vigour to government. He made changes to the cabinet and his tenure marked a sea change in the Dáil, as the veteran personalities made way for a new guard of professional politicians. By 1965, Frank Aiken was the only survivor of de Valera's government, the others having been replaced by the likes of Charlie Haughey, Patrick Hillery and Brian Lenihan Snr.

Rising Tides and the Father of Modern Ireland

'A rising tide lifts all boats.' This was the central tenet of Lemass's economic policy; that strengthening the country's economy would benefit all the people of Ireland, regardless of class. After almost three decades of protectionist policy, Lemass ushered in a new era. He built on proposals first mooted in the final days of de Valera's government to look outward, and to develop relationships with other countries (particularly in Europe) to attract foreign investment and encourage rapid industrial growth. This was a new Ireland.

On 10 November 1966, Lemass announced his retirement as Fianna Fáil leader and as Taoiseach in the Dáil, although he remained a TD until 1969.

A Pound of Tobacco and a Game of Rugby

Lemass was a prodigious pipe-smoker throughout his life, puffing through almost a pound of tobacco per week in his later years. When he retired as Taoiseach there was speculation that he was suffering from cancer; he wasn't, although his heavy smoking was to catch up with him eventually. In February 1971, Lemass became unwell while watching a rugby match at Lansdowne Road. He was rushed to hospital, where he learned that one of his lungs was close to collapse. Three months later, on 11 May, Seán Lemass died in the Mater Hospital. He was 71. After a state funeral, he was interred in Dean's Grange Cemetery.

Lemass's house on Palmerston Road was later owned and renovated by Fiona Healy.

Twice Taoiseach and a National Treasure

Another Taoiseach also had links with Palmerston Road. Dr Garret Fitzgerald (1926–2011), who was Taoiseach twice in the 1980s, lived at No. 61 Palmerston Road. He was the son of Desmond FitzGerald, the first Minister for External Affairs of the Irish Free State, following Independence in 1922. FitzGerald (an economist with the Economic and Social Research Institute for many years) was elected to Seanad Éireann in 1965 and was subsequently elected to the Dáil as a Fine Gael TD in 1969. He served as Foreign Affairs Minister from 1973 to 1977.

Fitzgerald was the leader of Fine Gael between 1977 and 1987. Various economic and political themes dominated his time as Taoiseach with emphasis on 'fiscal rectitude' vis-à-vis the economy, the hunger strikes in Northern Ireland (and the Anglo-Irish Agreement of 1985), and Irish Constitutional reform and the liberalisation of Irish society.

He fashioned our Future in so many Ways

Fitzgerald was prolific until the end. In his final years, he continued to make television appearances, he lectured at home and abroad, and he was the President of the Institute of International and European Affairs. He also maintained his column in The *Irish Times*, which he had done for some fifty-seven years, making him their longest-serving contributor. The 'newspaper of record' led the glowing tributes upon his passing: 'He was an extraordinary Irishman who fashioned our future in so many ways.'

President Mary McAleese described him as a man steeped in the history of the State who constantly strove to make Ireland a better place for all its people. 'His thoughtful writing, distinctive voice and probing intellect all combined to make him one of our national treasures. Above all, Garret Fitzgerald was a true public servant … Long after he departed active politics.'

He was affectionately known as 'Garrett the Good' as it was recognised that he wanted, first and foremost, to serve the people of Ireland selflessly, without fear or favour. It was said of him that Garret was an original and there are no copies or prints.

Sons, Guns and the Unfortunate Fursey

This elegant road was home to a number of other famous residents, including lawyer, dramatist and poet Donagh McDonagh, who lived at No. 9. He was the son of 1916 signatory Thomas McDonagh. His grandmother was Muriel Gifford, one of the Gifford Sisters from up the road at Temple Villas.

Mervyn Wall, author and Arts Council Secretary, was born in 1908 at No. 27. He was the author of *The Unfortunate Fursey*. This still popular book is a blend of satire, comedy and fantasy set in the tenth century where Fursey encounters sorcery, demons, witches, Vikings and the wealthy Festus Wisenuts.

The painters Moyra Barry and Fannie Beckett lived in No. 29 and No. 58, respectively. Another painter, Sara Cecilia Harrison (1863–1941), lived in No. 53. She was the first female City Councillor with Dublin Corporation.

Florence, Oscar and the 'Sweetest Years of my Youth'

Florence Balcombe, one-time girlfriend of Oscar Wilde, and later wife of Bram Stoker, author of *Dracula*, lived at No. 66 Palmerston Road. Earlier, during their two-year courtship, Wilde penned a love-poem to her called *Chanson*. He also gave her a gold cross. He described those years 'as the sweetest of all the years of my youth'.

The Irish Literary Revival and the Yeats Sisters

The famous Cuala Press was located in No. 46 for many years and the name 'Yeats' was inscribed on the door knocker from the 1940s until the late 1960s. The house itself was the home of Georgie 'George' Yeats, the widow of William Butler Yeats.

Founded in 1908 by Elizabeth (Lolly) Yeats, the Cuala Press played a pivotal role in the early twentieth-century Celtic Revival. Elizabeth had started her career working in London with the famous textile designer William Morris. In 1902, she and her sister Susan (Lily), an expert embroiderer, collaborated with their friend Evelyn Gleeson to establish a craft studio called 'Dun Emer', which was to become something of a hub for the burgeoning Irish Arts and Crafts Movement. Activities at Dun Emer included embroidery, tapestry, rug-making and printing. Lily oversaw the needlework department and Elizabeth managed the printworks (with support from her brother William).

Dun Emer and the Cuala Press

In 1904, the organisation was split into two sections: the Dun Emer Guild and Dun Emer Industries; four years later they were officially separated, and the Yeats sisters set up Cuala Industries, where they operated the Cuala Press and Susan's embroidery workshop. The Cuala Press was prolific and influential. Its objective was to promote the Irish Literary Revival and its writers, and between 1908 and its closure in 1946, the press published more than seventy texts. Forty-eight of these were by W.B. Yeats, but there were other very important names on the Cuala list, including Ezra Pound, Patrick Kavanagh, Jack B. Yeats, John Millington Synge, Lady Gregory and Louis MacNeice. The press was notable for its focus on new works, but it is particularly remarkable in that it was the only publishing house of the era to be run and staffed by women.

Yeats and the Door Knocker

Elizabeth Yeats died in 1940. Her two trusted long-time assistants, Esther Ryan and Marie Gill, continued the work of Cuala, then managed by Georgie Hyde-Lees – better known as Mrs W.B. Yeats. The last book by the original Cuala Press, *Stranger in Aran* by Elizabeth Rivers, was published in July 1946. In 1969 the press was revived by Georgie's children, Michael and Anne Yeats, in association with Liam Miller.

Ten Lives and the Shaking Hand of Dublin

Alfie Byrne (1882–1956) was an unprecedented ten times Lord Mayor of Dublin (1930–39 and 1954–55), and known as 'the shaking hand of Dublin' because of his political skills and friendliness, lived in No. 48 Palmerston Road. He was a popular politician and liked to cycle around the city on his sturdy bike. He was well dressed and sported a well-maintained waxed moustache. He had previously served both as an MP in the British House of Commons and as a TD in Dáil Éireann.

Architect of the Constitution of Ireland

At the Palmerston Park end of Palmerston Road there are two facing terraces consisting of nearly twenty houses that, although located on Palmerston Road, are known as Temple Villas and have a separate enumeration to copper-fasten this situation.

No. 3 was the home for many years of a barrister, legal scholar and diplomat, John J. Hearne (1893–1969), who is regarded by some as the architect-in-chief and draftsman of the 1937 Constitution of Ireland. Not only that, but he was legal advisor with the Department of External Affairs and worked with the Constitution Committee that drew up the 1922 Irish Constitution for the Provisional Government. Hearne was involved in every stage of the 1937 version, alongside Éamon de Valera. In his book *John Hearne: Architect of the 1937 Constitution of Ireland*, Eugene Broderick explains that 'his attitudes and concerns – especially with the protection of human rights in a period which saw the rise of dictatorships throughout Europe – governed the make-up of the fundamental law'. In 1950, Hearne became the first Irish Ambassador to the USA. In this role he began the tradition of presenting a bowl of shamrock at the White House on St Patrick's Day.

Temple of Intrigue and the Gifford Sisters

No. 8 Temple Villas was the home of the famous Gifford Sisters – Muriel, Sidney, Nellie, Kate, Ada and Grace. They were the daughters of middle-class Unionists Frederick and Isabella Gifford, and very prominent republicans (in addition, two were married to signatories of the 1916 Proclamation). Their father was a Catholic solicitor, their mother the daughter of a Church of Ireland rector, and from the 1880s the family lived at Temple Villas. There were thirteen children in the family; the first had died in infancy, then there were six boys and six girls. The six sons remained Unionist and Protestant but in later years four sisters converted to Catholicism (Kate, Muriel, Grace and Sidney) with the first three marrying Catholics.

Gifford household census, 1911. The family lived in Temple Villas, Rathmines.

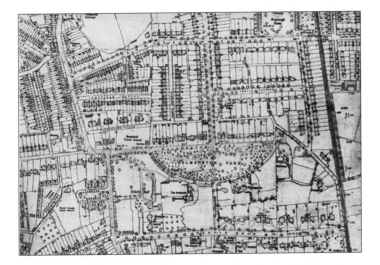

Map of Palmerston Park environs of Rathmines in early twentieth century. *Courtesy of DCC*

The Palmerston Grounds

In 1881, the Rathmines and Rathgar Township was offered a plot of land between Temple Road and Palmerston Road, known as the 'Palmerston Grounds' by the Lord and Lady Temple of the Cowper-Temple-Palmerston family. The plan was to convert the land to a public park. The renowned landscape and park designer William Sheppard was commissioned to design the new park and he followed a similar path to the one in Harold's Cross. This involved encircling the land with a railing surmounted on a granite plinth, planting trees, shrubs and enclosed flower beds, having paths for strolling and seats and red-bricked, internally tiled shelters for relaxing. A centre-piece involving a pond with a miniature cascading waterfall, was an attractive feature and today the fine park is an excellent example of a typical late Victorian park. Old photographs of the park show nannies pushing perambulators and children frolicking, often attired in sailor outfits, the fashion of well-to-do youngsters at the time.

A Unit of Electricity and the Boyle Medal

Palmerston Road brings us to the park and a road named after the park – Palmerston Park. The even larger houses overlooking this tree-packed park were built in the years following the completion of Palmerston Road in the 1860s. The renowned physicist George Johnstone Stoney lived at various times at No.3 Palmerston Road and No. 9, Palmerston Park. He originated the concept of a unit of electricity, calculated its size and named it the electron. In 1899, he was the recipient of the Royal Dublin Society's Boyle Medal, as he was considered to be the most eminent Irish scientist of his time.

A Doll's House and Ireland's Great Mansions

No. 20 Palmerston Park, was, for many years, the location for the Museum of Childhood replete with all types of toys from a bygone era associated with childhood. These included very intricate and finely crafted miniature doll's houses. One of these, Tara's Palace, is undoubtedly one of the world's most significant doll's houses. Sir Neville Wilkinson's celebrated Titania's Palace of 1907 inspired it. Meticulously constructed, it has taken over a decade to complete and work is still

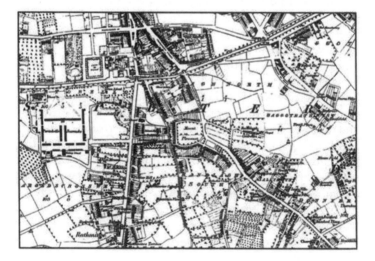

Rathmines and environs in 1837. *Courtesy of UCD Map Library*

ongoing. At precisely one-twelfth scale, it manages to pack in all the grandeur of the stunning mansions of eighteenth-century Ireland. It is inspired by three of these in particular: Castletown House, Leinster House and Carton. Every minute element in every room has been considered, right down to the artworks and finely crafted pieces of furniture.

Other attractions in the museum included a doll's house from the family of Lady Wilde (mother of Oscar), and 'Portobello', an antique from around 1700, which was previously owned by Vivien Greene. Vivien, who was married to the writer Graham Greene, was the leading English doll's house expert of the twentieth century.

The Childhood Museum and Tara's Palace, alas, were transferred from Rathmines to the Powerscourt Demesne in Enniskerry, Co. Wicklow, where they are still on view.

THE COWPER CONNECTION

The Virginia-clad Castellated Property

Palmerston Road is dissected north and south by Cowper Road, which stretches from Upper Rathmines Road to the LUAS line (Cowper Station) on the fringes of Ranelagh. Some very impressive houses are located here.

An outstanding property in the vicinity is Fortfield House, the distinctive Virginia-clad dwelling with its twin castellated turrets located on the corner of Cowper Road and Fortfield Gardens. It was originally built in 1740 but over time gave us the delightful and eclectic combination of Georgian and Victorian architecture. It was the first house built on the old lane that subsequently became Cowper Road. The name Fortfield might give us a clue to the Battle of Rathmines, 1649, and the possibility that the house was built on the site of a fort used in the battle.

The Mageough and Good Characters – no Drunks Need Apply

A hidden yet outstanding Gothic Revival enclave is the Mageough Home (1878) and the red-bricked dwellings in its immediate environs. There is also the fine Church of Ireland Victorian Mageough Chapel in the complex. The home was named in honour of Elizabeth Mageough who bequeathed in her will a sum of money for 'a suitable place for Protestant elderly ladies to live'. Not only that, however, these elderly ladies had to be 'aged females of good character and sobriety'. The current site was purchased from William Cowper Temple. It was located off Milltown Path, which ran from Portobello Bridge to the Nine Arches Bridge at Milltown. The name and a lane are still there in the area, linking Cowper Road to Temple Gardens. The first residents arrived in 1878. After the construction of Mageough Home, the Cowper, Palmerstown and Temple Roads evolved in its circumference.

Building Boom on Cowper

No. 5 Cowper Road would be an example of a trend – the sale of land to developers. According to a profile in the *Irish Times* (October 2015), 'The site was leased to builder Robert Eames in 1876 by the Rt Hon Frances Cowper Temple and the first owner of the then 5 Palanza Terrace, was one Joshua Doherty. He paid £400 for it in 1878. Several owners later, Palanza Terrace had become Cowper Road.'

Prestigious, Gracious and Exceptional

Cowper Road is an exclusive address. It is lined with splendid homes – many detached and most extremely elegant – built for the most part between the 1870 and the mid-1930s. There is a wealth of breathtaking splendour to absorb as you walk down Cowper Road and admire the red-brick, four-storey terraces, with their granite steps, iron railings and stained-glass front-door windows, and gaze upon the detached villas with their expansive gardens. It is easy to imagine that the elegance extends to the expansive interiors, blessed as they are with generous proportions and surely replete with period detail.

The Monied Classes – Building for Banks and Religious Institutions

Another interesting house is Beechdale, which was constructed by building contractor John Sisk for his family in the 1950s.

According to the *Irish Times* (February 2002), 'It was built from Dolphin's Barn brick and on 1.36 acres. It is tucked away at the end of a long beech-lined driveway. Set almost in the middle of the site, the house is surrounded by impressive gardens with magnolia, walnut and cherry trees. There is rear access onto Palmerstown Road.' The name Sisk is a by-word for construction in Ireland, and Sisk & Co. is the country's largest construction company. Having served an apprenticeship as a plasterer, John Sisk (b. 1837) set up his own business in 1859. His son, John Valentine, would become an equal partner and founder of John Sisk & Son. The first known contract was to build the Cork Distillery in 1868. In those early days, many of the building contracts were for banks and religious institutions – the sectors that had the money. Working mainly in stone and timber, many churches, convents, schools and banks built by Sisk still stand today. Yet it was the third John who really expanded the company on a national and international scale. After graduating as a civil engineer, he joined his father in the building of Cork City Hall in 1930. He moved to Dublin in 1937 to establish the company as a nationwide contractor. The family lived on Cowper Road, where John G. Sisk died.

William Pickering and Salubrious Homes

Building on Cowper Road continued sporadically until the late twentieth century and consequently the styles vary from detached villas to modern terraced houses. The builder, William Pickering, had a significant role in building of the fine house here in the early twentieth century. He was regarded as being one of the foremost builders of the time. His houses are known for their fine decorative work and interesting features, including double front doors, attractive stained glass, timber and railed verandas.

The Cowper Gardens scheme, which was completed in 1907, was advertised as something of a rural escape from the city. An ad in the *Irish Times* gushed: 'On the outskirts of Dublin, in country surroundings, viewing the Dublin mountains with the new Golf Links nearby … by train or tram you can reach central Dublin in a few minutes.'

8

THE GROSVENOR CONUNDRUM

DIAMONDS, DIADEMS AND CONUNDRUMS

Just beyond Rathmines Garda Station, the road divides. Left is the Rathgar Road, right is Grosvenor Road. Yet, Rathgar Road itself starts back at the major junction and so part of it is in Rathmines. Moreover, some say Grosvenor Road is in Rathgar, some say it is in Rathmines. Some just don't know. Some even say that part of it is in one or another of these fine suburbs. Despite the confusion, and according to some that seem to definitely know, from the Charleville Road end of Grosvenor Road to the Diamond intersection at the Baptist church, we are in Rathmines. From that junction, the road curves around to

Rathgar Castle near Rathmines as drawn by Gabriel Beranger, 1769. *Courtesy of NLI*

Rathgar Road, beside the Church of the Three Patrons – that part of the road is Rathgar. It all boils down to the belief held by some that what actually distinguishes Rathgar from Rathmines comes down to just one word – 'Posh'.

Rathgar's pretentiousness – at least that was others' perception – is illustrated in Jimmy O'Dea's song, 'Thank Heavens for Rathgar'. The legendary O'Dea, pantomime stalwart in Dublin's Gaiety Theatre for decades until the early 1960s, and the man who gave us (with Harry O'Donovan) the inimitable typical Dublin fish hawker, 'Biddy Mulligan, the Pride of the Coombe', often sang:

> There are some quite decent suburbs, I am sure.
> O Rathmines is not so bad or Terenure.
> In Dartry they are almost civilised.
> O we have heard of spots like Inchicore,
> But really don't know where they are.
> For, thank heavens, we are living in Rathgar.

GRIMWOOD'S AND THE DEVELOPERS

For many years until the mid 1850s Grimwood's Nurseries was located close to the junction of Rathgar Road, Grosvenor Road and Rathmines Road. The nurseries occupied approximately 15 acres of land. This was an excellent location for Grimwood's, as the underground River Swan ran close by, essential for the growing of plants and vegetables to supply some of Dublin's needs. A painting by Cecilia Nairn in 1817 shows a pathway leading to the nurseries with a river and the Dublin Mountains in the background. Even before the 1850s, however, Dublin's developers had started to plan for the building of Grosvenor Road on the Grimwood's lands.

BEATER, BECKETT, CARSON – GOTHIC, SWISS AND BYZANTINE INFLUENCES

Grosvenor Road has a variety of Victorian architecture with houses designed by some of Dublin's renowned architects including Edward Henry Carson (father of the Ulster Unionist leader, Edward Carson, who was born at the family's home on Harcourt Street), George Palmer Beater, James and William Beckett (William was the grandfather of Samuel Beckett). Some of the Grosvenor Road houses actually date from as early as 1840, with Rosetta at No. 26 built in that year, Grosvenor House at No. 2 built in 1848 (although there is another newer Grosvenor House across the road!) and Rathmore at No. 19, built in 1852. The majority, however, date from the 1860s. The grey picturesque Baptist church overlooking the Diamond, at the junction of Grosvenor Road and Grosvenor Place, was built in 1859.

Beside the church, No.17 is Gosford (home to William Acheson, related to the Earls of Gosford, a goldsmith, watchmaker and jeweller with premises in Grafton Street). It was designed by Edward Carson, using Gothic, Swiss and Byzantine influences. No. 18, St Michael's House, is a fine detached ornate red-brick building. St Michael's is part of an organisation that has been catering for the needs of Down's syndrome children since 1955, having been founded by Patricia Farrell, a farmer from Co. Westmeath. No. 20 is of a different yet elegant style, having been designed by George William Beater, who used the Gothic Revival style.

THE REV. BENSON AND THE FAMOUS MCBIRNEY'S DEPARTMENT STORE

Across from the church, the detached No. 15, called St Brendan's and dating from 1860, also overlooking the roundabout, is built on a substantial plot of land and attracted much attention and offers (up to 15 million euro) during the Celtic Tiger era. Woburn House was built in 1864, as was Tavistock at No. 39. Thornville at No. 16 dates from 1862. Westminster at No. 10 dates from 1860 as does Wakefield at No. 7. Alma House at

No. 18 dates from 1860. Two three-storey semi-detached houses, Nos. 26 and 27, dating from *c*.1859, with flights of steps leading up to the front doors, occupy the corner facing toward Rathgar Road. No. 27 was the home for many years of the McBirney sisters, from the family that owned the famous department store, McBirney's, located on Dublin's Aston Quay.

ANATOMY DICK AND THE SPIKEY GOTHIC

Particularly attractive are the line of ten detached villas, Nos. 66 to 75, stretching from the Rathmines end of Grosvenor Road up to the Diamond. Most of these were built in the mid-1860s, although Laurel Bank at No. 70 dates from 1906 and Hughenden at No. 67 dates from 1896. No. 73 was once home to Professor Andrew Francis ('Anatomy Dick') Dixon. Rev. Charles William Benson (1836–1919) headmaster of the famous Rathmines School (beside the Catholic church) lived from 1865 to 1880 at 65 Grosvenor Road. Further along the road, Nos. 53–56 were described by the architectural historian Jeremy Williams 'as the most ambitious Gothic Revival speculative terrace built in the Dublin suburbs; designed in the rather spikey Gothic idiom employed by both A.G. Jones and E.H. Carson'. These houses have four levels and with prominent bow windows. Entrances are accessed by flights of granite steps.

FANLIGHTS, KINGS HEADS AND HALOS

An unusual feature of houses Nos. 35–39 is the line of small sculpted heads, one above each of the front-door fanlights. Each of these mostly male heads has a different expression, and one wears a crown. The only female head is adorned with a halo-like piece. The story is told that the reason for only one female head is that when the builder was refurbishing the property in 1997, he was unable to find a replacement head for the missing male one and had to opt for the present head instead.

The old Fenian, John O'Leary, lived at different addresses in Rathmines and Rathgar, including for a time at 30 Grosvenor Road.

THE SQUARE, THE MISSING HOUSES AND THE MACKINTOSH MAN

Grosvenor Road is linked to Grosvenor Square by Grosvenor Place and part of Leinster Road, all of which are in Rathmines. No. 11 Grosvenor Place was home to Francis and Francis Sheehy-Skeffington family for many years.

Passing the homes of the Haslams and Countess Markievicz on Leinster Road brings us around the corner to the secluded Grosvenor Square. There are three-storey houses on two and a half sides of the square and two storeys on the other one and a half sides. Houses were originally built for the officers of the Portobello Barracks which was beside the site. The square was built in phases with the result that certain house numbers are not included, e.g. Nos. 70–73. The numbers here leap from 69 to 74. Most of the houses on this side of the square are two-storey and single-fronted, including Nos. 75 and 76. However, four of the houses are double-fronted, from No. 77 to No. 80, hence the missing four numbers which would have corresponded with four more single-fronted houses.

The square was home to a number of luminaries including Hollywood film director Rex Ingram who was born at No. 58. No. 67 was the home for many years of George Russell. Born in Armagh in 1867, George Russell's family moved to Dublin in 1878 and Russell spent much of his boyhood in Grosvenor Square. The actor Brendán O'Dúill (1935–2006) lived at No. 63. He was known for films such as *Into the West* (1992), *The MacKintosh Man* (1973) and *The Lost Hour* (1982). He was a renowned singer, brought out a number of LPs and was involved with Comhaltas Ceoltóirí Éireann. He also appeared in *The Riordans* and many other RTÉ productions.

The square is also the site of the Kenilworth Bowling Club, Stratford Lawn Tennis Club and the Rathmines Chess Club. The Portobello GAA Club is adjacent in the grounds of Cathal Brugha Barracks.

WHITHER? RATHGAR ROAD AND RATHMINES

From the New Road to The Thatch

Rathgar Road begins its journey in Rathmines and a number of businesses and Rathmines Garda Station are located on it. It is nearly a mile long and is a very straight and uniform road, dating from *c*.1815. It was constructed to link Rathmines with Highfield Road and Roundtown Road (Terenure Road East) and then on in the direction of Rathfarnham Road.

Despite construction of the road, which began at the beginning of the nineteenth century, for some years it remained without a single dwelling to 'relieve its monotonous straightness or interrupt the view of the open pastoral country through which it passed', according to the historian Weston St John Joyce, in his *Neighbourhood of Dublin*. It was first shown on Taylor's Map of 1816 as 'New Road', without any houses indicated. It continued to be known by locals as 'the new road' and Highfield Road, 'the old road'. When it was being built, at the section where it met the upper end of Highfield Road, now the village, there then stood a few thatched cottages and an inn, the latter a favourite hostelry for country people going in and out of town by that route. In time, this group of houses became known as 'The Thatch', and was referred to by that name for many generations of dwellers of the outlying parts of south County Dublin.

From Exclusively Rural with Villas to Expansion with Fairy-like Rapidity

Rathgar Road beyond Rathmines remained an exclusively rural district until the 1840s when a few detached residences began to make their appearance. Some of the oldest properties would date from the 1830s/1840s and even earlier, including the villas in Auburn Villas and Belleville Avenue. Early houses were modelled on the Georgian style, and dwellings, as in Rathmines, are noted for their richly decorated features, excellent plasterwork and joinery.

Local resident Michael Barry, in his book *Victorian Dublin Revealed*, noted that *The Dublin Builder* rhapsodised about Rathgar Road in 1859 that 'villas, single and semi-detached, terraces etc., are springing up with an almost fairy-like rapidity, and the green sward speedily gives way to macadamised roads with populous thoroughfares'. However, what we see today as a nice straight, uniform road did not happen all at the same time. As with Rathmines, it was built villa by villa or terrace by terrace. There were times when building gathered apace, again, as in Rathmines, particularly in the 1860s and 1870s.

9

REVOLUTIONARIES AND THE IRISH REVIVAL

RATHMINES – CRUCIBLE FOR CHANGE

Despite being, and maybe because of being, a predominantly Protestant and staunchly Unionist enclave in Dublin, Rathmines housed many Irish nationalists and republicans. All were anxious to assert Ireland's right to return to being an independent country. It has been said that the history of Ireland and the struggle for Irish independence may be seen in microcosm in the area. From the Celtic time of the 'Rath' and

The birth of 'The Nation'.

the coming of the Normans, to the Massacre of Cullenswood in 1209 and the Battle of Rathmines in 1649; from Henry Grattan and Irish legislative independence to the Robert Emmet rebellion of 1803 (name commemorated at the end of Grove Road on Harold's Cross Bridge); from the Young Irelanders, the Post-Famine era, the Fenians and Parnell the 'Uncrowned King of Ireland', to the Irish Revival, the 1916 Rising and the War of Independence: all the pivotal events in Ireland's history and its assertion of its nationhood were mirrored in, or played out on the stage that is Rathmines.

JAIL JOURNAL AND THE YOUNG IRELANDERS

John Mitchel (1805–75) was a nationalist activist, solicitor and political journalist who became a leading member of the Young Ireland movement and the Irish Confederation in the 1840s. The Young Ireland movement was a romantic nationalist group composed mainly of graduates of Trinity College who came from middle-class and traditionally non-sectarian families. Over time, however, Mitchel's views

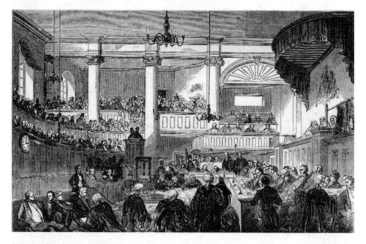

Trial of John Mitchel in Green Street Courthouse, Dublin, in 1848. He lived at various houses in Rathmines.

Newgate Gaol, Dublin, where Young Irelander, John Mitchel of Rathmines, was detained.

were strengthened by the anger that he felt in relation to the Great Famine and England's disdain and disregard for the poor of Ireland. He established a newspaper called *The United Irishman*, and he used this as a means to promote a revolution by the proletariat. He was living with his family at 8 Ontario Terrace, when he was arrested in 1848. He was subsequently elected to the British House of Commons only to be disqualified because he was a convicted felon (due to his striving for the social and political improvement of his fellow citizens in Ireland).

The 1848 Young Irelanders' Rebellion was a resounding failure, after which Mitchel was sent to Tasmania. He escaped to America in 1853, where, somewhat incongruously, he was a supporter of slavery and took the side of the South in the Civil War. Later, he moved to Paris, where he remained and worked with the Fenian Brotherhood there until a falling out with the leadership in 1865. In 1875 Mitchel returned to Ireland, and shortly before his death he was elected MP for Tipperary. His text entitled *Jail Journal: or Five Years in British Prisons* (published 1876) remains a hugely influential work in Irish nationalism.

THE BIRTH OF A NATION AND THE FUTURE PRIME MINISTER

Another Young Irelander lived in Rathmines. Charles Gavan Duffy (1816–1903) lived at Holmeville, behind the Town Hall,

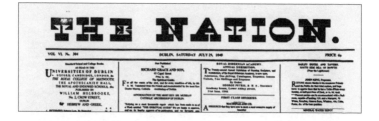

and later across the road in Leinster Square. A very able man of letters, he was a nationalist who left an indelible mark on Irish and Australian politics. He was born in Monaghan Town, where his father was a Catholic shopkeeper, but following the death of his parents he was raised by his uncle Fr James Duffy in Castleblaney. He was educated in Belfast and he was admitted to the Irish Bar in 1845, by which time he was already deeply involved in Irish political and literary circles.

Duffy founded *The Nation* with Thomas Osbourne Davis and John Blake Dillion. He was also the editor, and it was under his stewardship that the publication began to make waves as a rebellious faction.

From Monster Meetings to the House of Lords

The Nation's vociferous support for Repeal of the Act of Union led to Duffy's arrest. He was convicted of 'seditious conspiracy', relating to the organisation of the 'Monster Meeting', which was to take place in Clontarf. He secured his release thanks to an appeal to the House of

Young Irelander, Charles Gavan Duffy, who lived in Rathmines.

Lords, and he was, in fact, elected to the House of Commons in 1852 (representing the constituency of New Ross). In 1850 Duffy had established the Tenant Right League to lobby for reform in the Irish land system and to protect the rights of tenants. Shortly after he was elected to the House of Commons, the government introduced a land bill in accordance with the principles of the League.

From Australia to Marriage in Paris

The land bill was passed by the House of Commons in 1853 and 1854, but was blocked by the House of Lords, and so in 1855, feeling more disheartened at the state of affairs than ever, Duffy announced his intention to retire. He felt that he had let his constituents and countrymen down, and he saw little hope of Irish independence. The following year he resigned from the House of Commons and he emigrated to Australia with his family, settling in the new colony of Victoria. Following a successful career in Australian politics, though not easy, Duffy eventually retired to the south of France in 1880 where he continued to support the Irish Home Rule struggle. While in his seventies, he married for a third time in Paris in 1881 and went on to have four more children (he had six with his second wife).

THE DUFFY DYNASTY AND ROGER CASEMENT'S TRIAL

One of his sons, by a previous marriage, was John Gavan Duffy, a Victorian politician between 1874 and 1904. Another son, Sir Frank Gavan Duffy, was Chief Justice of the High Court of Australia 1931–35. His daughter Louise was an Irish republican present at the 1916 Easter Rising. She was an Irish language enthusiast who founded an Irish language school for girls near Rathmines – at Cullenswood Avenue, Ranelagh. Yet another son, Mr Justice George Gavan Duffy (born 1882), was an Irish politician and later (from 1936) a judge of the Irish High Court, becoming its President from 1946 until his death in 1951. In 1916, it was he who defended Roger

Casement at his trial for treason in London. A grandson, Charles Leonard Gavan Duffy, was a judge on the Supreme Court of Victoria, Australia.

THE CABBAGE GARDEN REVOLUTION

Fenian John O'Leary (1830–1907) lived at different times on Grosvenor Road (No. 30) and Leinster Road (No. 40). He identified with the views advocated by Young Irelander Thomas Davis and met the future Fenian leader James Stephens (who lived at Leinster Square) in 1846. He associated with other Young Irelanders including Charles Gavan Duffy, James Fintan Lalor and Thomas Francis Meagher. After the failure of the 1848 Tipperary Revolt (known variously as 'the Battle of Widow McCormack's *cabbage* plot', or the 'Cabbage Garden Revolution', such was the small size of the effort in Ballingarry), he was imprisoned from 5 September 1849. He had attempted to rescue the leaders from Clonmel Gaol. A further uprising in Munster on 16 September 1849 gave him an opportunity to escape from prison, which he took.

Sir Charles Gavan Duffy (1816–1903) was a Young Irelander and one of the founders of *The Nation* newspaper. In later life he was an Australian statesman. He lived at Holmeville and Leinster Square, Rathmines.

A Street in Ballingarry, 1848

Ballingarry, Co. Tipperary, site of the 1848 Young Ireland's Insurrection. John Mitchel lived at Ontario Terrace and elsewhere in Rathmines.

WITH O'LEARY IN THE GRAVE

O'Leary was arrested on 14 September 1865. He was convicted of high treason and sentenced to twenty years' penal servitude. Nine of these were spent in England, before he was exiled to Paris in 1874. He remained there until the Amnesty, and in 1885 he returned with his sister, poet Eileen O'Leary. They quickly became significant figures on the cultural and nationalist landscape, and they moved in the same Dublin circles as the

likes of W.B. Yeats and Maud Gonne. John O'Leary died on 16 March 1907, and is buried in Glasnevin Cemetery alongside James Stephens, for whom he had been best man in 1864.

Fenian James Stephens.

Contemporary cartoon image of the Fenian, James Stephens.
He lived at No. 2 Leinster Square.

OF LIBERTY AND BONDAGE – THE BOLD FENIAN MEN

A contemporary and neighbour of O'Leary was another
Irish patriot, James Stephens (1825–1901), railway engineer,
republican nationalist, and founder of the Fenians. He lived at
No. 2 Leinster Square. Upon joining the Young Irelanders in 1847,
Stephens quickly became a prominent figure. He was injured in
the 1848 rebellion but was able to flee to France, where, with
other exiles, he established the Irish Republican Brotherhood.
They were known as 'Fenians', like their counterparts in the

US (who organised in 1858), and the aim of both factions was the formation of an Irish Republic. When Stephens returned to Ireland in 1856, he set about creating and managing Fenian cells around the country. However, there was a bounty on his head and he was forced to flee to America again. He returned to Ireland once more in 1861 and continued to fight for independence.

THE POET, THE PATRIOT, THE PAINTER – ON FUMBLING IN THE GREASY TILL

The inscription on the Celtic cross on John O'Leary's grave, next to that of James Stephens, reflects the lives of both these brave Fenians: 'A day, an hour of virtuous liberty is worth a whole eternity of bondage.'

O'Leary is also immortalised in one of W.B. Yeats' greatest works, 'September 1913':

> What need you, being come to sense,
> But fumble in a greasy till
> And add the halfpence to the pence
> And prayer to shivering prayer, until
> You have dried the marrow from the bone;
> For men were born to pray and save;
> Romantic Ireland's dead and gone,
> It's with O'Leary in the grave.

Today, the National Gallery of Ireland holds a painting of John O'Leary, painted by Jack B. Yeats, brother of the poet. Both the patriot and the painter had lived in Rathmines (Grosvenor Road/Leinster Road and Charleville Road, respectively).

THE REBEL COUNTESS OF LEINSTER ROAD

Countess Constance Markievicz was born in 1868 into the wealthy Anglo-Irish Gore-Booth family, who divided their time between townhouses in Dublin and London, and the majestic Lissadell House in County Sligo. Constance studied at the Slade

School of Art in London and later moved to Paris, where she met her future husband, Kazimierz Dunin-Markievicz, a Polish painter and a self-styled Count. They moved to Dublin in 1903, and in 1912, the couple settled at No. 49b Leinster Road, where they raised their daughter Maeve and Kazimierz's son from his first marriage, Stanislaus. From 1908, Constance was heavily involved in nationalism, and during the 1913 Lockout, she paid for and distributed food for the families of workers, and she established a soup kitchen to feed schoolchildren.

THE SPARK OF SPEAKER CONNOLLY

The Labour leader and Irish Citizen Army founder James Connolly (with his family) shared the large house with the Markieviczs from 1913 and 1916. Consequently, in the lead-up to the 1916 Rising, it was a popular rendezvous for those involved in the nationalist and labour movements and the Fianna (Irish Volunteers). The 'Surrey House Clique' was a term often ascribed to those coming and going to the house. *The Spark* and the *Workers' Republic* were printed here. Soon the house became a de facto headquarters for the Fianna. Neighbours recall Countess Markievicz having a firing range in her garden.

THE FIRST WOMAN ELECTED TO PARLIAMENT

Having fought in the 1916 Rising, Countess Markievicz was arrested and sentenced to death. As a woman, her sentence was commuted to life imprisonment, unlike other leaders who were executed. In 1917, she and all the remaining 1916 prisoners were released. In 1918, she was elected to the British House of Commons, the first woman to be elected to Parliament. As a nationalist, she refused to take her seat. Instead, the hugely successful Sinn Féin, having ousted the Irish Parliamentary Party, set up its own parliament in Dublin, called 'Dáil Éireann'. Constance was appointed Minister for Labour and was one of the first women in the world to hold a cabinet position.

TWO GIRLS IN SILK KIMONOS
– DEATH OF A COUNTESS

When Fianna Fáil was founded in 1926, Countess Markievicz was quick to get involved, even chairing the inaugural meeting in the La Scala Theatre. The summer of the following year she was re-elected to the Dáil on behalf of the party, but she sadly died on 15 July before she could take up her seat. She was 59 when she died, on 15 July 1927, possibly of tuberculosis (contracted when she worked in the poorhouses of Dublin) or complications related to appendicitis. Her estranged husband and daughter and beloved stepson were by her side. She was buried in Glasnevin Cemetery. Éamon de Valera, the Fianna Fáil leader, delivered the funeral oration.

William Butler Yeats wrote a poem, 'In Memory of Eva Gore-Booth and Con Markievicz', in which he described the sisters as 'two girls in silk kimonos, both beautiful, one a gazelle'.

NORA CONNOLLY O'BRIEN, THE
ASGARD AND THE CALL OF THE HARP

Another influential woman during and after the 1916 Rising was Nora Connolly. The second daughter of James Connolly, she was born in Edinburgh in 1893, and the family moved to Dublin when she was 3. When she was 9, the family moved to New York, before returning to Ireland again in 1910, this time to Belfast (Nora had, in fact, gone a year earlier). Leaving school at the age of 13, she worked in a milliner's, and then as a dressmaker, all the while developing her passion for politics. Nora had had an interest in socialism since childhood, having witnessed her father's impassioned speeches, and as a teenager she became the business manager of *The Harp*, the newspaper of his Irish Socialist Federation.

In 1914, as the First World War was beginning in Europe, plans were taking shape for a rebellion in Dublin, and Nora and her sister Ina helped to transport arms and ammunition from Childers' Asgard in Howth to hiding places around the city. The women were rewarded with a rifle each, but Nora's involvement did not end there. She was sent to America to inform her father about the planned Rising, due to take place at Easter 1916, and there she met Roger Casement, who was fundraising for the Irish Volunteers and spreading awareness of their cause. She also travelled to Belfast in an effort to drum up support. On the morning of the Rising itself, she cooked breakfast for the leaders at Liberty Hall, which she described as a 'rare privilege'. In 1922 she married Seamus O'Brien, a courier for Michael Collins whom she met while working undercover in Boston.

FROM CLEEVES TOFFEES TO WE SHALL RISE AGAIN

After the Civil War ended, Nora and Seamus lived in a rented flat near Belgrave Square. At this time, Seamus was working for Cleeves confectioners. In the 1930s, the couple had a newsagent's-cum-lending library in Rialto, but the onset of the Second World War and subsequent rationing forced its closure. Nora then worked for the Post Office and for Rathmines College, but politics were never far from the O'Briens' minds.

Nora and Seamus were passionate members of the Labour Party, and Nora served three terms in the Seanad between 1957 and 1969. Hers was a varied career; she received an honorary Doctorate in Law, helped to commemorate the fiftieth anniversary of the Easter Rising, and she was heavily involved in the restoration of Kilmainham Gaol, where her father was executed in 1916. In addition, she was a prolific author, writing extensively about her father's life and the nationalist struggle. Her final work, *We Shall Rise Again*, was published in 1981. Nora died that same year, on 17 June, aged 88.

LISSENFIELD HOUSE AND THE HEART OF THE REVOLUTION

Lissenfield House, on Rathmines Road (facing the church), was the home for many years of General Richard Mulcahy (1886–1971), another staunch activist in the struggle for Irish

Independence. Mulcahy had an illustrious career; he fought in the Rising, served as Chief of Staff of the IRA during the War of Independence, and succeeded Michael Collins as commander of the pro-Treaty forces in the Civil War. After the war, Mulcahy remained unforgiving of the anti-Treaty side; he ordered that members found with arms faced execution (Kevin O'Higgins was also responsible in this regard). In the end, seventy-seven anti-Treaty activists were executed. Not too long afterwards, on the east-facing wall of the church, across from his house, one of the workers carved the numbers 77 on one of the blocks. Post-independence, Mulcahy served as leader of Fine Gael.

THREE SISTERS, A HEART SPECIALIST AND FASHION DESIGNER

Meanwhile, in 1920 Mulcahy had married Min Ryan, the former fiancé of 1916 signatory, Séan MacDiarmada. Min was a sister of Kate and Phyllis Ryan, successive wives of politician and later President of Ireland, Séan O'Kelly. The sister's brother was another politician, James Ryan. Min was an activist in Cumann na mBan during the revolutionary period.

Their children became successful in diverse careers, among them Risteárd, a leading Irish cardiologist and campaigner on heart health; Neillí, one of the country's most important fashion designers (among myriad achievements, she designed the uniforms for Aer Lingus in 1962); and Seán, who was a structural engineer and an artist.

TEA WITH G.K. CHESTERTON AND LIFE ON ACHILL ISLAND

The dapper, red-haired and red-bearded Darrell Figgis (1882–1925) was born in Palmerston Park, but raised in India. His was a short and tragic life. He worked as tea broker in London and Calcutta, 1898–1910, with his father's prosperous tea-importing business. However, his heart was elsewhere, and his published poems *A Vision of Life* (1909), with a preface by

G.K. Chesterton, secured him a position as a reader for Dent, 1910–13, and eventually an editor. He wrote fiction including *Broken Arcs* (1911) and then returned to Ireland in 1913 when he bought a cottage on Achill Island, having come under the influence of W.B. Yeats and the Celtic Revival. There he met the painter Paul Henry and here he was also sworn into the Irish Volunteers. Meanwhile, he edited a volume of stories of William Carleton (Rathgar/Ranelagh resident) and wrote a play *Queen Tara* that was produced by F.R. Benson at the Abbey in 1913.

FROM THE ARAN ISLANDS TO TRAGEDY

He was involved with Bulmer Hobson in organising the famous Howth gun-running, following a meeting on 8 May 1914 at the home of A.S. Green in which he was instructed to buy arms in Germany for the Irish Volunteers ('Let us buy arms and so at least get into the problem'). During the War of Independence, as Honorary Secretary of Sinn Féin, 1917–19 he was imprisoned twice. Meanwhile, over these years he continued his writing with a new novel, *Jacob Elthorne* (1914) and *Children of Earth* (1918), about life on the Aran Islands. He became a TD for Dáil Éireann in 1918, following the landslide Sinn Féin victory. He was a prominent member of the First Dáil and helped draw up the Irish Free State's first Constitution. There is a plaque to him in the 'Constitution Room' in Dublin's Shelbourne Hotel, commemorating his chairmanship of the Constitution Committee.

His final years were very difficult – his wife Millie died by suicide, seemingly traumatised by an attack on her husband by the IRA during the War of Independence; his girlfriend died from blood poisoning following an abortion in London. Shortly afterwards, in 1925, he was found dead in a London guesthouse.

THE GIFFORD SISTERS AND
THE MARRIAGE OF MINDS

The story of Grace Gifford is one of the most poignant scenes associated with the Easter Rising. She married Joseph Mary Plunkett in Kilmainham Gaol mere hours before his execution, but what is perhaps less well known is her family's already long-standing involvement in the struggle for Irish independence before this. Grace grew up in a large house on Palmerston Road (Temple Villas), where she was the second youngest of twelve. Although raised Protestant and Unionist, Grace and five of her sisters converted to Catholicism and the nationalist cause. The Gifford women were wholly committed to the fight for freedom, and supported the movement in Ireland and the USA, never shirking from accompanying challenges and tragedy. Muriel married another 1916 leader, Thomas MacDonagh, who had been known to walk around Rathmines and Rathgar wearing a kilt. This did not please the Unionist-minded residents who, it was said, 'trembled with rage'.

Cover of a book by Grace Gifford, one of the six Gifford Sisters of Temple Villas, Rathmines.

Marriage Certificate of 1916 leader, Joseph Mary Plunkett and Grace Gifford of Rathmines.

'I SEE HIS BLOOD UPON THE ROSE' – UNLIKELY REBELS

Grace Gifford was an artist and cartoonist. It was her interest in Catholicism which led Grace to Joe Plunkett, who was intensely devoted to his religion as well as to the Republican cause. His sacrificial romanticism was expressed in poems such as: 'I see His Blood Upon the Rose'. Their wedding was reported all over the world. Grace, like Sarah Curran before her, who had loved Robert Emmet, had become a tragic symbol of Ireland's struggle with England.

'STIFLING AND SNOBBISH' AND THE MILK BOTTLES

The Gifford sisters were well acquainted with the leaders of the Rising (Muriel married Thomas MacDonagh in 1912), and they were also proponents of the Irish Women's Franchise League, the country's first militant suffrage organisation. In addition to Grace and Muriel, there was Nellie (later Donnelly), Sidney (later Czira), Kate and Ada. During the Easter Rising, Nellie fed volunteers at the Royal College of Surgeons garrison. Grace and Muriel were the first of the sisters to be widowed, their husbands being signatories of the proclamation who were subsequently executed. Grace's younger sister Sydney became a writer, describing the Rathmines of their childhood as a stifling and snobbish place where anyone who had an original thought was written off as eccentric.

Grace's last years were marred by poor health. On 13 December 1955, a neighbour noticed that she had not collected her single bottle of milk or her post from outside her flat in South Richmond Street, Portobello. She had died alone, in bed. She was buried with full military honours at Glasnevin, near the Republican plot.

PORTOBELLO BRIDGE AND 'FIVE MINUTES TO GET OUT'

Portobello played its own part in the frenzied events of the Easter Rising. The Irish Citizen Army sent a company to the bridge to seize a delaying position. The group was led by one James Joyce (not the author), who knew the area extremely well as he worked in Davy's Bar there. He chose the bar as their outpost, but when the unit burst in they found the eponymous Davy was less than impressed. He sacked Joyce on the spot, giving him one week's notice. Joyce, unfazed, simply gave the landlord five minutes to get out of his own pub.

MURDER MOST FOUL

Rathmines was the site of a number of deadly incidents during the Revolutionary period. During the Civil War, Seamus O'Dwyer, an important activist in the War of Independence, a local Sinn Féin Councillor and supporter of the new Irish Free State government, was shot dead in his shop on Rathmines Road (beside Edward Lees) in January 1923.

RIDDLED WITH BULLETS

Mysterious Shooting Of Young Harold's Cross Man

Residents of the Upper Rathmines road had an appalling experience yesterday morning when they came out of doors about 6.30, and found a young man's body lying bathed in blood, and apparently riddled with bullets, at the edge of the footpath outside the walls of the Tranquilla Convent.

Cutting from *Freeman's Journal*, 24 March 1923.

Further up the main road, there is a memorial with a Celtic cross on the wall of Tranquila Park, the former Carmelite convent, to Thomas O'Leary, who was murdered at the spot in 1923, also during the Civil War. It was unveiled ten years later. He was a young IRA man attached to the 4th Battalion. He was found riddled with twenty-two bullets – one for every year of his life – at the gates of Tranquila Convent.

IRA member Timothy Coughlan was killed on the evening of 28 January 1928 on Dartry Road, opposite Woodpark Lodge. Coughlan was regarded as having been associated with the assassination of Government Minister Kevin O'Higgins in 1927.

10

THE BARRACKS AND
THE GENERALS

FROM PORTOBELLO TO CATHAL
BRUGHA BARRACKS

Cathal Brugha Barracks stretches from Grove Road, fronting
the Grand Canal, to the main entrance at Military Road, off
Rathmines Road Lower. It was opened in 1815, under the
name Portobello Barracks, and it was here that Francis Sheehy-
Skeffington, Thomas Dickson and Patrick McIntyre were
executed on 26 April 1916. The guard room in which the men
were killed without trial is now a visitors' centre. The barracks
became the headquarters of the National Army under Michael
Collins in 1922, and today it is home to the 2nd Eastern Brigade,
the 2nd Infantry Battalion, the Defence Forces School of Music
and the Military Archives.

REGIMENTS AND RIFLES –
GOLDIE'S DRAGOONS

In its first century, the barracks was significantly developed;
the church was added in 1842, the canteen in 1868, and in
1887, surrounding land was purchased, extending the complex
to a total of 36 acres. The first inhabitants of the barracks
were the 6th Dragoon Guards, but over the years it has also
accommodated the Royal Scots Fusiliers, the Royal Munster
Fusiliers, the Sherwood Foresters, the Derby Regiment, the
Durham Light Infantry, the Warwickshire Regiment, the

Middlesex Regiment, the East Lancs Regiment, The Buffs Regiment, the Wiltshire Regiment, the Royal Inniskilling Fusiliers and the Royal Irish Rifles.

HYDROGEN AND CYANIDE – GUNS, BULLETS AND BEDROOMS

In 1817, William Sadler became the first person to fly successfully across the Irish Sea. He achieved this amazing feat in a hydrogen-filled hot air balloon from Portobello Barracks to Holyhead, North Wales. Sadler was the son of James Sadler, an English aeronaut who specially came to Dublin to attempt the feat (unsuccessfully, five years previously). Sadler's balloon was 70ft in diameter and it took six hours to cross the Irish Sea and he eventually landed in a cornfield at Anglesey, 2 miles inland from Holyhead.

Unsurprisingly, security in the area was increased around the time of the Fenian Uprising. According to an 1867 report in the *Irish Times*, an innocent young man from Bloomfield Avenue was arrested and accused of breaking and entering while walking his dog; he was acquitted, to some bemusement, considering her was carrying a gun and eighteen bullets at the time!

The barracks were the scene of a dreadful crime on 27 December 1873. Gunner Colin Donaldson was found dead on the bed of one Anne Wyndford Marshall in the apartment she shared with her husband. It transpired that Donaldson had been poisoned with hydrogen cyanide that had been purchased by Mrs Marshall a few days before, but, despite the overwhelming evidence against her, she was found not guilty on 10 February 1874.

SHAMROCK, SHOOTINGS AND THE MURDER OF SHEEHY-SKEFFINGTON

On St Patrick's Day 1916, the Countess of Limerick visited the barracks, bringing shamrocks for the troops, but during the Rising just a few weeks later these same troops killed numerous civilians in the area, and three influential prisoners. Thomas

Dickson, Patrick McIntyre and Francis Sheehy-Skeffington (editor of *The Irish Citizen*) were shot without trial on 26 April 1916, creating widespread outrage.

Soldiers from the British 11th East Surrey Regiment arrested Sheehy-Skeffington on 25 April. A renowned pacifist, he was on his way home to No. 11 (now No. 21) Grosvenor Place when he was apprehended without explanation and taken to the barracks. He was deemed an enemy sympathiser, and that night he was brought along by a raiding party to the home and business of Alderman James Kelly. Kelly, who was mistakenly believed to be a rebel, lived just down the hill from the bridge, and it is from him that Kelly's Corner takes its name. Led by the now-infamous Captain J.C. Bowen-Colthurst of the Royal Irish Rifles, the gang destroyed Kelly's shop and arrested two of his customers, as the hostage Sheehy-Skeffington looked on. As the troops retreated to barracks, Sheehy-Skeffington watched in horror as they murdered two random, innocent civilians.

THE SACKED OFFICER AND THE INSANE BOWEN-COLTHURST

The next morning, Bowen-Colthurst ordered the execution of Sheehy-Skeffington and the two customers from Kelly's shop. These unlucky individuals were Thomas Dickson (a disabled Scotsman) and Patrick McIntyre. They were both journalists. All three died by firing squad, and an immediate effort was made to conceal the killings, with Bowen-Colthurst being offered the command of a regiment in Newry. His commanding officer, Sir Francis Fletcher Vane, did make a valiant effort to have Bowen-Colthurst held accountable for the murders, but saving face was more important to the army; Vane was swiftly discharged, although it is thanks to him that these despicable actions were made public. 'An Irishman's Diary' in the *Irish Times* (23 February 2004) revealed that official papers stated that Vane was 'relegated to unemployment owing to his action in the Skeffington murder case in the Sinn Féin rebellion'.

At a subsequent inquiry, Bowen-Colthurst was deemed to be insane and he spent eighteen months in Broadmoor Prison.

Today, the barracks' visitor centre is dedicated to the memory of Skeffington, Dickson and McIntyre.

Troops from the barracks were involved in a number of other incidents during the Rising and the War of Independence. On one such occasion, Major Vance led troops against the South Dublin Union, where Cathal Brugha was the second-in-command of the defending forces. In 1920, an incident of fisticuffs that became known as the 'Battle of Portobello' began with a crowd of locals embroiled in a fight with British soldiers. The latter had insisted on playing a song called 'The Kings' at the City Theatre. A running battle ensued, which culminated at Portobello Barracks.

KELLY'S CORNER AND THE LORD MAYOR OF DUBLIN

Alderman Thomas J. Kelly (1868–1942), in whose tobacconist shop the episode began, was a Home Ruler and an influential member of Dublin City Council in the early decades of the twentieth century. Suspected of having nationalist sympathies, he was arrested after the 1916 Rising and imprisoned in England.

Following his release after being in Brixton for eighteen days, he became more active in politics and was elected as a Sinn Féin MP for the Dublin St Stephens's Green constituency at the 1918 general election. He was elected Lord Mayor of Dublin in 1920 but his health prevented him from taking office. In 1930, he joined Fianna Fáil and was elected as a TD at the 1933 general election for Dublin South. He remained a TD and councillor until his death in 1942. Among his lasting achievements were the introduction of social housing to replace slums, a greatly improved public library service, and the foundation of the Municipal Gallery of Modern Art.

THE TIME OF THE GENERALS

The Irish National Army took control of Portobello Barracks on 17 May 1922. Comdt General Ennis, OC Second Eastern Division, took over from Major Clarke of 5th Battalion and

Worcestershire Regiment, and one Captain McManus became OC. As army headquarters, Portobello Barracks was a hive of activity, full of influential people. Michael Collins was, of course, Commander in Chief, with Mulcahy as his deputy and Minister for Defence, Sean McMahon as Quartermaster General and Gearoid O'Sullivan as Adjutant General. It was from here that Collins left Dublin on 12 August 1922 for his tour of the south of Ireland. He was never to return. It was renamed Cathal Brugha (1874–1922), who was a leader during the 1916 Rising, Minister for Defence in the First Dáil, and who lived on Rathmines Road for a time.

CANDLE-MAKER'S COURAGE AND OBSTINACY

Born in Fairview in 1874 and educated at Belvedere College, Cathal Brugha was a man of many talents. He was known for his skills with languages and flair for football, hurling and boxing. He was a candle-maker by trade but was to become an Irish hero, thanks to his involvement in republican politics and the conflict of the early decades of the twentieth century.

In 1913, Brugha had become a lieutenant in the Irish Volunteers, and by the Easter Rising, he was Vice-Commandant 4th Battalion of the Dublin Brigade at South Dublin Union under Eamonn Ceannt. He was severely injured during the Rising, and was left with a permanent limp, and after this time he became a TD (and was Minister for Defence for a period). When the Dáil met on 22 January 1919, he was chosen as the first President of the Republic, but by April he had stepped aside to make way for Éamon de Valera.

Cathal Brugha died on 9 July 1922, having been shot by Free State troops on O'Connell Street two days before in a tense Civil War showdown. Following his death, many tributes were paid to Brugha from both sides of the political divide. In his 1958 biography of the general, Rex Taylor relays that of Michael Collins:

Because of his sincerity, I would forgive him anything. At worst, he was a fanatic though in what has been a noble cause. At best, I number him among the very few who have given their all ... that this country should have its freedom. When many of us are forgotten, Cathal Brugha will be remembered.

THE RED HOUSE, EVIE HONE AND ULYSSES

Other interesting features of the barracks include St Patrick's Garrison church, which is adorned by a stained-glass altar window by Evie Hone (1849–1955) and The Red House, which was General Michael Collins' private residence when he was Commander in Chief.

James Joyce includes a mention of the barracks in his writings: 'He had a good slice of luck, Jack Mooney was telling me, and over that boxing match Myler Keogh won again that soldier in the Portobello barracks. By God, he had the little kipper down in the county Carlow he was telling me ...' (*Ulysses*, Chapter 2, Lestrygonians episode, James Joyce).

11

SAINTS AND SINNERS

THE GOTHIC AND THE GLORY – GROSVENOR ROAD BAPTIST CHURCH

Built in 1859, this fine grey structure with a pinnacle facade on Grosvenor Road is an interesting example of Gothic Revival architecture. The main entrance to the church has a fine arrangement of arches, with an attractive towering facade. Standing on the corner of Grosvenor Road and Grosvenor Place, the church is attributed to the renowned architect Edward Henry Carson, and was built by English Baptists as a Baptist church for the area. It was used for some time by the Plymouth Brethren but returned for use by the Baptist community in 1942.

Rathmines Gospel Hall brochure cover. *Courtesy of Rathmines Gospel Hall*

RATHMINES – REFUGE FOR SINNERS

The most distinctive feature of the Rathmines skyline is the copper dome of Mary Immaculate Church. From many vantage points in areas surrounding Rathmines, particularly Ranelagh, Portobello and Camden Street, one could not fail to be captivated by the impressive and towering green dome. Moreover, this famous landmark is also visible from the Dublin Mountains.

There was much debate about where the parish should have its church. Finally, in 1824, a little over two acres of unoccupied land situated between the canal and Richmond Hill were purchased from the Earl of Meath, Lord Brabazon.

STICKY FINGERS BRABAZON AND THE FOUNDATION STONE

The Brabazons' connection to Ireland began when William Brabazon was sent to Dublin in the early 1530s by Henry VIII as his Vice-Treasurer during the Reformation. He was to ensure that the spoils of the dissolution and confiscation of the monasteries and churches would go into the Crown's coffers. He was subsequently known as 'Sticky Fingers' Brabazon because of his self-aggrandisement at the expense of the Crown. Years later, in 1824, a descendant, the Earl of Meath, sold this plot of land on the border of Rathmines and Ranelagh for the building of a church. Lord Brabazon, the Earl, laid the foundation stone.

This Gothic Church measured 90ft long by 37ft wide with a height of 37ft. It cost approximately £5,000 and it took five years to build, not helped by the settlement problems with one of the walls. Archbishop Murray consecrated the church in 1830. Some of the land originally purchased was eventually sold to obtain funds to finish the interior of the church. All was well for a number of years until, however, by the middle of the nineteenth century, the expansion of Rathmines and the consequent increase in the Catholic population necessitated enlargement of the church.

THE ITALIANS, THE GREEKS
AND THE RUSSIANS

Years later, in July 1848, a visiting missionary priest, Fr Gentili of the Order of Charity, described some beautiful churches he had observed in Italy and called for the building of a new church in Rathmines. In September of that year, a public meeting was held to discuss the proposition to build a bigger church. It was decided to retain the existing location with the church facing the main Rathmines Road. On 18 August 1850, Archbishop Murray laid the foundation stone of a new church. It was to be built to the Byzantine model, with a Greek cross formation. This was significant, as it was the first design of its kind in the Archdiocese of Dublin since the Catholic Emancipation of 1829.

Patrick Byrne designed the new church, constructed around the original building. He was the leading architect of Catholic neo-classical churches in post-Catholic Emancipation decades. The church rates as one of Byrne's masterworks and can be considered of national architectural significance. The stone used in the construction was from Kimmage and Donnybrook, and the masonry work was carried out by John Lynch of Mountpleasant Avenue. There were a number of highly skilled Dublin craftspeople involved, including William Hughes of Talbot Street, who managed the construction of the roof and the dome, and Messrs Hogan and Connolly of Pearse Street (then Brunswick Street), who did the plasterwork.

THE PORTLAND PORTICO, THE
EMINENT STATUE AND GOLD PAINT

In 1856, the church was completed with the exception of the portico and was dedicated by Archbishop Cullen on 19 June. It was a truly impressive occasion with sixteen bishops and 200 priests present at the ceremony. Work began on the grand Portland stone portico in 1878 and was completed in 1881, to coincide with the church's twenty-fifth anniversary. It was designed by architects O'Neill and Byrne, who were members of the parish, and the work was carried out by Meade & Son, who were also locals. It is a stunning addition to the church, with its four towering columns and intricate detailing. It is crowned by the statue of Our Lady of Refuge, that had previously been set into the façade's central alcove. She is flanked by statues of St Patrick and St Laurence O'Toole, which stand on either end of the portico. The gilt letters stand for the Latin 'Deo Optimo Maximo', and beneath this, also in Latin, it says 'Dedicated to God the Most High under the invocation of Mary Immaculate, Refuge of Sinners'.

Many present and former parishioners will remember the Rathmines Folk Group, which was founded in 1972 and is still going strong to this day.

HOLY SMOKE – THE TRAGIC FIRE OF 1920 AND THE MANSION HOUSE MEETING

As explained by Louise Buckley on *In Rathmines* (inrathmines. blogspot.com), on the morning of 26 January 1920, the sacristan arrived at the church to prepare for 7 a.m. Mass only to discover that the switch panel was on fire. Apparently, someone had used silver paper on a fuse to prevent it from blowing. The only problem was that everything else went on fire instead. The sacristan raised the alarm, but the altar was already aflame, and the blaze was spreading rapidly. Nothing could be done, and at 9 a.m. the dome collapsed, crashing to the ground. Inside, only the shrine of Our Lady of Perpetual Succour and the sacristy were unscathed. Luckily, the original external walls remained intact.

As news of the fire spread, Archbishop Walsh and Alderman William T. Cosgrave (later President of the Executive of the Irish Free State and leader of Cumann na nGaedhael) of Dublin Corporation called during the day to offer sympathy to the parish priest. The next day a heavy gale damaged two stained-glass windows valued at £1,000.

The following week, on 5 February 1920, a public meeting to discuss the rebuilding of the church was held in the Mansion House. The Lord Mayor presided and those present included the Archbishop, the Lord Chief Justice and members of Dublin Corporation. Renovations quickly got under way and it was re-opened only five months later on 4 July 1920, the main structure of the church having survived intact. This speedy work was greatly facilitated by the fact that the main structure of the church was still standing, and virtually undamaged.

THE MAD MONK AND THE GREEN DOME

The church's dome had been completely destroyed and was replaced with a large copper dome that had been built some time previously for a different client. This dominates the skyline when viewed from far and near. It is even visible from the Dublin Mountains. The dome, built in Glasgow, Scotland, was destined for a Russian Orthodox church in Petrograd (now St Petersburg), but the political and social upheaval there following the two 1917 Revolutions, including the Bolshevik, caused it to be diverted to Dublin. The Revolutions witnessed the quick demise of the Tsars and the concomitant influence on the royal family of the infamous Rasputin, known as 'The Mad Monk'. Were it not for the nefarious influence of Rasputin the Mad Monk on the Tsarina, the skyline of Rathmines and Dublin might well have been radically different.

CHALLENGE TO THE ASCENDANCY

As a particularly ambitious example of Catholic church building, it is of historical significance as a document of social change, demonstrating the emergence and increased confidence of a Catholic middle class in the latter half of the nineteenth century, in what was a bastion of Protestant and Unionist influence and control.

Rathmines Gospel Hall on Upper Rathmines Road.

JOYCE, THE CIVIL WAR AND THE SEVENTY-SEVEN MEN

James Joyce's parents married in this church in 1880. The family ended up living on nearby Castlewood Avenue for a number of years.

It has been suggested that during the War of Independence some members of the IRA used areas of the church, not used by the public, for hiding weapons. During the 1920 fire, alarm bells rang, not just for the fire brigade, but for Volunteers, who hurriedly accessed the church to retrieve guns. There is also a persistent story that the number 77 was put into stonework on the eastern external wall by a disgruntled bricklayer in 1923, during the Civil War. The figures were supposed to have been carved in stone above a stained-glass window – on an arched lintel on the eastern-facing side of the church. The view was that it was in protest at the seventy-seven executions authorised by the fledgling Irish Free State Government during the Civil War. General Mulcahy's house, Lissenfield, was directly across the road from the church. He had given the order that anti-Treaty activists found carrying guns were to be executed.

FROM MYTHS TO ENIGMAS

However, on closer inspection of said wall, there is no such carving. Furthermore, there is also supposed to be a similar carving on the northern-facing flank of the church. Again, there is no such evidence, unless one wishes to misinterpret a few scratches or the brick and mortar alignment in certain parts of the wall as such numbers. The only conclusion that can be arrived at in these circumstances is that the story is nothing more than a myth, possible peddled by disgruntled survivors of the turbulent era.

Of real significance, however, in that eastern external wall, nearer ground level, is a clear carved image of the number seven with a line through its middle (7). This enigmatic number, carved with such meticulous care, has also been on wall for decades and has lent itself to numerous interpretations, including Biblical, mathematical, astrology, literature, music and sport, but no widely accepted view prevails.

THE BLACK CHURCH AND THE BOARD OF FIRST FRUITS

The Holy Trinity church is now nearly 200 years old. Originally built in 1828, it has been modified and expanded over the years. It is a landmark structure holding a pivotal position where a number of roads off Upper Rathmines Road intersect including Belgrave Road, Purser Gardens, Castlewood Park, Church Avenue and Cambridge Road.

The Church of Ireland's Holy Trinity Church was consecrated on 1 June 1828. Designed by John Semple in the Gothic Revival style, it was built with Black Calp, which is a local limestone that turns black in the rain, garnering it the nickname 'Black Church' (one of two in the city, the other being located at St Mary's Place). The church had an ominous appearance on wet nights, and local children feverishly shared the theory that if you walked around it three times backwards, after midnight and under a full moon, you would meet the Devil himself.

Sketch of Holy Trinity Church, late nineteenth century. This is the work of John Semple, perhaps the most enigmatic of Irish architects.

JOHN SEMPLE AND THE GOTHIC REVIVAL STYLE

Semple shares the same name as his father who was also an architect, and both worked for the Board of First Fruits. John Semple junior also designed The White Church, Monkstown, Church of Ireland, St Maelruan's in Tallaght and also the Round Room in the Mansion House. Semple's 'late English Gothic' style of architecture is now regarded as being way ahead of its time.

Some of the windows are stained glass and it has one steeple which holds the bell. The front door is strikingly narrow – maybe a parable in timber? There are also a number of interesting and ornate Great War and Second World War rolls of honour and other memorials located within the church. The church is surrounded by gravel and railings.

THE CHAIN-SMOKING SINGING PRIEST

The 'Singing Priest', as Father Michael Cleary was called, lived at Mount Harold Terrace, Leinster Road, for a number of years until his death in 1993. This short terrace of red-bricked houses was built for officers at the nearby Portobello Barracks. Fr Cleary was a popular radio and TV personality, as well as being a newspaper columnist. In addition, he was a published author and released two albums, hence the 'Singing Priest'. A larger-than-life character, he was one of the best-known priests in the country in the 1970s and '80s, and a man of significant influence. He put this power to good use in Dublin, where he was dedicated to working towards change in impoverished inner-city communities. Fr Cleary was a frequent sight in the Rathmines area, walking around, chain-smoking, with a newspaper under his arm.

However, after his death in 1993, *The Phoenix* claimed that Cleary had fathered two children with the woman who had been acting as his housekeeper at Mount Harold Terrace. The first, it was reported, was given up for adoption, while the other child lived with his parents in a secret family.

12

GHOSTS, SCRIBES AND ARTISTS

AN IMPORTANT PART OF DUBLIN'S LITERARY TRADITION

In 2010, Dublin received the UNESCO designation 'City of Literature', and many would argue that Rathmines is the literary heart of this erudite city. The area has been, for many decades, the first port of call for creatives of every discipline, but especially with writers and journalists, and so it is no surprise that Rathmines has an excellent library that is a hub for everything literary.

One of the most outstanding and landmark buildings in Rathmines is Rathmines Public Library, located on Rathmines Road, across from the Town Hall. As well as the library, the building complex also holds the former Rathmines Technical Institute (with RTI still displayed on the steel gates on the Leinster Road entrance) and which is now the College of Music. This college has expanded and now incorporates the former College of Commerce (now Rathmines College) which has moved across the road to new premises in the former Town Hall as well as occupying a number of houses further up Leinster Road.

Since it opened in 1913, Rathmines Library has been part of the very fabric of the village. Standing opposite that other instantly recognisable Rathmines landmark, the Town Hall, the library is a grand edifice, with its classical façade and shining William Morris window.

THE MUNIFICENCE OF THE STEEL MAGNATE

The library has the words 'Public Library' carved in stone high above its front entrance. Below, and written on a blackened copper plaque over the door, are the words, 'Erected through the munificence of Andrew Carnegie, esq., L.L.D.' Andrew Carnegie (1835–1919), of Scottish origin, started off as a telegraph messenger boy, over time evolved into an American steel magnate, and is often regarded as one of the richest people ever. He even surpassed John D. Rockefeller at one time. He was a renowned philanthropist and gave away $350 million dollars to charities, foundations and universities. He believed the rich should use their wealth to improve society. His name lives on in Carnegie Hall in New York and in library buildings such as the one in Rathmines. Providing opportunities for easy access

to books was a huge part of his philanthropic philosophy.

US postage stamp image of the renowned steel-magnate, multi-millionaire and philanthropist Andrew Carnegie of Carnegie Steel in Pittsburgh. He contributed to the building of many libraries, often called Carnegie Libraries, and one of these is Rathmines Library.

ARKLOW BRICK AND AN ORNAMENT TO THE TOWNSHIP

The library was built in the Baroque style in 1913, designed to fit in with the style of the Town Hall. In Arklow terracotta brick and terracotta facade, it is another one of the many stunning buildings Rathmines has to offer. Rathmines had adopted the Public Libraries Act in 1887 to mark the diamond jubilee of Queen Victoria. Rathmines was the only authority in Ireland to do so, and lost no time in establishing a library committee.

The first library in Rathmines was situated at No. 53 Rathmines Road. It was opened in June 1887 and was soon so popular that it required bigger premises. It was moved to No. 67 Rathmines Road in 1899, and there it remained for fourteen years.

It was then decided that Rathmines needed a new, purpose-built library – an 'ornament to the township'. The new library, which was designed by Bachelor & Hicks of Dublin, was opened on 24 October 1913. Halfway up the beautiful double staircase is this window designed by William Morris with the word 'Literature' on it. William Morris was a famous English artist and designer who also designed beautiful furniture and fabrics.

The library offered many services, including a lending department, and a special room in which to read newspapers, which were then prohibitively expensive for most people to buy regularly. One service it did not have originally, however, was a children's library. This was soon remedied by Mary Kettle and other women town councillors; they understood the benefits it would bring to local children and precipitated the opening of such a facility in 1923.

HORSE RACING BE DAMNED! NO SMUTTY BOOKS HERE!

According to Séamas O'Maitiú in his book, *Dublin's Suburban Towns 1834–1930*:

> under the Library Acts it was not necessary for members of library committees to be councillors and such bodies in Ireland were noted for their clerical representation. This was the case in Rathmines where local clergymen were seldom absent from the library committee. Reading material was closely vetted and the committee felt obliged occasionally to censor the material made available to the readers.

He noted that the committee had also instructed the librarian to 'expunge as far as possible all sporting news relating to horse racing from the newspapers provided for the public in the library'.

Retrieved leaflet publicising the opening of Rathmines Library. *Courtesy of Rathmines Library*

During the Second World War, the basement was used as a bomb or air raid shelter. Over the years, speakers such as the poet W.B. Yeats (1926), Douglas Hyde (1928) and the feminist Hanna Sheehy-Skeffington (1931) were invited to give talks. Douglas Hyde also gave talks. He was known as 'An Craoibhín Aoibhinn' (The Pleasant Little Branch), was a leading figure in the Gaelic Revival, and went on to become the first President of Ireland.

The library also houses a plaque from the Princess Cinema. Originally called the Rathmines Picture Palace, the Princess was opened shortly before the library, on 24 March 1913.

GREAT WRITERS AND ARTISTS

The Joyce Family of Castlewood Avenue

Renowned the world over, the modernist icon James Joyce is considered by many to be Ireland's greatest ever writer. He was born on 2 February 1882 at No. 41 Brighton Square in Terenure; after spending his first two years there, he moved with his family to No. 23 Castlewood Avenue, where he stayed until he was 5. It was here, it was said, that he wrote his first words, and speculation continues as to whether 'take me up to Monto' were some of those. However, the family fell on hard times, forcing them to move away from the area. Joyce would never live in Rathmines again. He left the country with Nora Barnacle in 1904, and, as is widely known, he spent the rest of his life in mainland Europe. But Dublin was never far from his mind and his canon of work is rich with detail about the city. *Dubliners* and *Ulysses* in particular are lasting classics of Dublin literature.

The Rebel's Wife and the Troubled House

Rosamund Jacob was born in 1888 in Waterford and lived there until 1920, and while hers is not a well-known name today, she was an influential and dedicated activist and writer throughout her life. She fought tirelessly for the suffrage, republican and socialist movements, all the while writing for adults and children. Jacob moved to Rathmines *c*.1942, living first at Belgrave Square and later at No. 17 Charleville Road. She died in 1960, leaving behind a number of published works, as outlined by Dublin City Libraries in their 2011 online biography of Jacob:

> Her first novel was called Callaghan and was published in 1915, but she struggled to make a living from her writing. Her other publications include The Troubled House, based on the experience of Ireland's Civil War; The Rebel's Wife, which was loosely based on the life of the wife of Henry Joy McCracken, and a children's book, The Raven's Glen, which was published just before her death.

That Myriad Minded Man – George Russell's Irish Homestead

Born in Armagh, George Russell (1867–1935) moved to Dublin with his family in 1878, living for a time at No. 67 Grosvenor Square. He began his working life as a clerk but soon moved on to become the director of the Irish Agricultural Organisation Society. He was for many years the editor of *The Irish Homestead*. Russell adopted the pseudonym 'Æ', a name that became instrumental in literary circles from the 1890s to the 1930s. Æ wore many hats – poet, mystic, commentator – but he was most admired for his nurturing influence on emerging artists of all kinds. Russell and his wife, Violet, lived on Mountpleasant Avenue, which was a hub for the creative set, and later they resided at No. 17 Rathgar Avenue.

Yeats, Joyce and Mary Poppins

In 1902, Æ took a young James Joyce under his wing, introducing him to his most important contemporaries, including Yeats. In return, Joyce immortalised his mentor in *Ulysses*; Æ makes a cameo in the episode 'Scylla and Charybdis', discussing Greek philosophy and dismissing Stephen's musings on Shakespeare.

Æ's Sunday evening salons were an important part of the Dublin literary and artistic scene.

Interestingly, one of the people who was at his bedside when he was dying was Mary Travers (along with Oliver St John Gogarty and Con Curran), the author of *Mary Poppins*! He had published some of her poetry in earlier years and they had maintained a lifelong friendship. He is buried in Mount Jerome Cemetery, Harold's Cross.

Francis Sheehy-Skeffington 1878–1916 – An Irish Citizen

Raised in Cavan and educated in Dublin, Francis Skeffington adopted the surname of his wife Hannah Sheehy upon their marriage in 1903. The couple, who lived at No. 11 Grosvenor Place (now No. 21), were spirited activists and proud nonconformists, with alternative views on a wide range of issues, including religion, women's rights, and capital punishment. Together they founded the suffragist *Irish Citizen* newspaper. Despite his fervent pacifism, Francis was tragically murdered in Portobello Barracks during the Easter Rising under orders from Captain John Bowen-Colthurst.

From the Fire Station to Gur Cake

While he is more famously associated with the Liberties, writer Eamonn Mac Thomáis (1927–2007) was in fact born in Rathmines. His father was an officer in the fire brigade, and Eamonn came into the world in a room above the village's fire station. Sadly, his father died when Eamonn was just 5, after which the family relocated to Inchicore. He wrote best-selling books that are bursting with Dublin imagery and memories, and he was particularly interested in immortalising the city's singular language, customs and characters. His works included *Me Jewel and Darlin' Dublin*, *Janey Mack Me Shirt is Black*, *The Labour and the Royal*, and *Gur Cake and Coal Blocks*.

Tombs, Tomes and Sixteen Dead Men

A daughter of eminent scientist, politician and writer George Sigerson, Dora Sigerson Short (1866-1918) was another woman who played an important role in the Irish Literary Revival. She spent her early childhood at No. 17 Richmond Hill and showed an early talent for poetry. In adulthood she was a prolific writer of poems and ballads, and she is perhaps best known for 'Sixteen Dead Men', her tribute to the leaders of the Easter Rising. Dora lived in Dublin until she married her husband Clement K. Shorter, when the pair relocated to London, and Dora stayed there until her death in 1918. In paying tribute to her friend, writer Katharine Tynan suggested that Dora had died of a broken heart caused by the 1916 executions. Her close ties to the events of 1916 are commemorated in the memorial that she designed for Glasnevin Cemetery.

Sigerson's Secrets and Sealed Cylinders

Dora Sigerson Short was also a gifted sculptor, and upon her death she bequeathed money for the erection of the 1916 memorial on her own burial plot. It was completed in the late 1920s. Hewn from white Carrara marble and inspired by Michelangelo's *Pietà*, it depicts Mother Ireland cradling one of Ireland's lost warriors – a 1916 rebel with more than a passing resemblance to Pádraig Pearse.

In 2007, a secret was discovered within during the process of dismantling the monument for restoration. Upon removing the canopy, workers found a long lead cylinder built into the masonry. It was found to be a time capsule and handed over to government officials. There has been much speculation as to its contents, but it was left unopened and later returned to its original hiding place. According to Stephanie Breen, Assistant Librarian in the Department of Early Printed Books and Special Collections at Trinity, 'it is believed to contain a vellum parchment embossed with the names of all those who died in the Rising'.

Politicised Life of Propagandist of Palmerston Park

The son of a tea merchant, Darrell Figgis (1882-1925) was born in Palmerston Park. The family moved to Sri Lanka (then Ceylon) shortly after, returning when Darrell was 10. He worked in the family business until his first book of poetry was published in 1909, after which he devoted himself to his writing and to Republicanism. Figgis published plays, novels and criticism, but as time went on his passion for politics eclipsed his writing. From 1914 he was active in Republican military activity, and he spent much of 1916 to 1919 in jail. Post-Treaty, he was involved in drafting the 1922 Constitution and he stood for election, but he died tragically in 1925, having taken his own life in rented rooms in London.

The Cruiser – Trenchant and Outspoken Critic

Politician and journalist Conor Cruise O'Brien (1917–2008), known as 'the Cruiser', is as well remembered for his unconventional views as for his writings. A master of culture and controversy, he was born in Rathmines (his mother was Kathleen Sheehy, sister of Hannah Sheehy-Skeffington) but he spent a great deal of his adulthood abroad. He was an MEP for Ireland in 1973 and later a diplomat, which included a posting to the Congo. Over time, his politics swung from the left to the right, and in the later 1970s he left politics altogether to work in journalism. He was Editor-in-Chief of *The Observer* from 1979 to 1981, and he published many history books and biographies (his subjects included Parnell, Camus, Thomas Jefferson, and himself).

Nursing Republicans – Strong and Noble-Minded

Born at No. 12 Richmond Hill, Rathmines, Annie M.P. Smithson (1873–1948) had dreams of becoming a journalist but instead she trained as a nurse in London and Edinburgh. She worked for a time in County Down before returning to Dublin in 1906. She soon converted to Catholicism and became deeply involved in the nationalist cause. She was a committed member of Cumann na mBan and a canvasser for Sinn Féin, and after the Treaty, she was arrested for nursing wounded Republicans. She was imprisoned in Mullingar but later rescued by friends posing as members of the Red Cross. From 1929 to 1942, Smithson was deeply involved in the Irish Nurses Organisation, and as a nurse and midwife she worked tirelessly amongst the poor in the tenements of Dublin. Years later, she recounted her time working in Mercer's Hospital, York Street, and a girl she called 'Mary Mercer' who was so fond of cats that she made 'cat holes' in the hospital walls for the convenience of the cats to come and go!

She Walked Like a Queen in Times of Peril

While Smithson did publish journal articles, she is undoubtedly best known for her fiction. Her famously romantic novels have a strong nationalist subtext that made them extremely popular around the country. Her first novel, the best-selling *Her Irish Heritage* (1917), was dedicated to those who died in the Easter Rising. In all she wrote nineteen novels, each plot more elaborate and romantic than the last. Many featured autobiographical threads, including her own doomed relationship with a married doctor, but all her heroines are impressively strong-willed and principled. Her bibliography includes such titles as *Carmen Kavanagh, The Walk of a Queen, The Laughter of Sorrow, The Light of Other Days* and *The Weldons of Tibradden*. She kept writing up until the time of her death, by which time she had become a best-selling novelist. In all, she published sixteen novels and an autobiography. In her book *In Times of Peril: Leaves from the Diary of Nurse Linda Kearns*, she charted Easter Week, 1916 and the War of Independence through one of its heroines.

Other best-selling novels included *The Marriage of Nurse Harding, By Strange Paths* and *Leaves of Myrtle*. She is buried in Whitechurch Cemetery, overlooking the city.

The Jail Journal of a Young Irelander

John Mitchel was born in County Derry in 1815 and moved into the Rathmines area in the 1840s, residing at No. 8 Ontario Terrace. Mitchel was a prolific political commentator, and his home in Rathmines was a hive of activity, particularly for the Young Irelanders. He was the editor of *The United Irishman*, which made him a person of interest to the authorities. He was subsequently arrested and the paper suppressed, and after the failed uprising he was transported to serve his four-year sentence

The Widow McCormack's House, Ballingarry, Co. Tipperary, site of the 1848 Young Ireland's Insurrection, also known as 'the Cabbage Garden Revolution'. John Mitchel lived at Ontario Terrace and elsewhere in Rathmines.

abroad, first in Bermuda and then in Tasmania. He escaped in 1848 and fled to the USA, where he remained until 1875, when he returned to Ireland and he died that same year. While most of Mitchel's work was historical, he is best known for his journalism and his account of his imprisonment. *Jail Journal*, first published in 1854, became nothing short of a sacred text for Republicans.

From Richmond Hill to Strumpet City

James Plunkett Kelly, better known simply as James Plunkett, was a Dublin-born writer who spent much of the late 1940s and early '50s living at No. 25 Richmond Hill. During this time, he worked in the Rathmines offices of the Gas Company, and in 1952 his first work was published – a radio play entitled *Dublin Fusilier* (March 1952). He wrote more radio plays, as well as short stories, but he is best known for *Strumpet* City, a novel inspired by the Lockout of 1913. It was published in 1969, and its evocative depiction of poverty and the plight of the working class made it an instant and lasting success. Plunkett died in Dublin in 2003, aged 83.

Japanese Ghost Stories and Haiku Poetry

Born in Lefkada (the origin of his middle name), one of the Greek Ionian Islands, of an Irish father and Greek mother, writer Lafcadio Hearn (1850-1904) spent many years in Rathmines, living with his aunt Sarah Brenan. From 1852 to '53 he stayed with her at No. 30 Leinster Square, and from 1853 to '55 they lived at No. 3 Prince Arthur Terrace. Hearn had a fascination with foreign cultures, and when he came of age he embraced world travel. In 1869, Hearn moved to the USA, where his writing talents found him work as a journalist. He had a particular love for New Orleans, and wrote extensively about his experiences there, but it is for his life in Japan that he remains best known. He moved to the country in 1890, adopting the name 'Koizumi Yakimo'. He adored Japan and was massively inspired by the culture. He wrote about all aspects of Japanese life – their customs, religion, poetry, and even superstitions – and he is often credited with introducing the culture to many Westerners. He is also said to have given the West the expression 'the Tsunami Effect', which derived from some of his work.

From the Rathmines Medical Hall to the Dublin Magazine

Poet Seamus O'Sullivan was born James Sullivan Starkey at No. 7 Charleston Avenue in 1879. His family owned a successful pharmacy at No. 30 Rathmines Road, known as the Rathmines Medical Hall; James worked for the business, but came to deeply resent it as he grew up and became drawn to the literary set. He spurned the wealthy suburban Rathmines scene and adopted his maternal grandmother's name in order to sound more Gaelic. He published his first volume of poetry in 1905, and he went on to publish fifteen books in his lifetime. His greatest legacy, however, is considered to be *Dublin Magazine*, which he first published in 1923 and ran for more than thirty years. The publication prided itself on supporting emerging talent, and it printed early pieces by such esteemed writers as Patrick Kavanagh and Samuel Beckett. In 1929, O'Sullivan married the artist Estella Solomons, and the coupled moved to Rathfarnham.

Fishing, Travel and Wine – Gaelic Traditions

Stephen Gwynn (1864-1950) was a writer, teacher and nationalist politician. He was born in Rathfarnham, but spent a lot of his childhood in Ramelton, County Donegal, where his father served as parson for many years. This period in the rural idyll of Donegal is credited with instilling in Gwynn his love of Irish traditions. Gwynn graduated from Oxford with first-class honours, then spent time teaching in France, where he honed his writing skills. He kept close ties with Ireland and became involved in the literary revival, and upon his return he threw himself into politics. In 1904, Gwynn served as MP for Galway, and he remained in politics until the 1920s, when he turned his full attention to writing. He published numerous books on a wide variety of subjects, including history, humanism, travel, fishing and wine. He died on 11 June 1950 at his home at No. 23 Palmerston Road.

The Years Flew by with the Hungarian

The journalist Sidney Czira (1889–1974) was the youngest member of the Gifford family that lived at No. 8 Temple Villas. Two of her sisters, Grace Gifford Plunkett and Muriel Gifford MacDonagh, married leaders of the Easter Rising who were subsequently executed. Sidney was similarly captivated by the nationalist cause and the associated Celtic Revival. She wrote from her youth, using the pseudonym John Brennan for published pieces. She moved to the USA in 1914, and there she married a Hungarian man called Arpad Czira. All the while she practised her journalism, and she continued doing so upon her return to Ireland in 1922. She also moved into radio broadcasting for 2RN (later Radio Éireann). Her 1974 memoir, *The Years Flew By*, is a fascinating account of her exciting life and career.

Acerbic Eye for Female Experience in Ireland

Although born and raised in County Monaghan, novelist and short-story writer Evelyn Conlon has lived in Rathmines for a number of years. Her debut collection of stories was released in 1987, and since then she has published six books and contributed to and edited many more. An elected member of Aosdána, she has assumed the role of writer-in-residence in many libraries and colleges around the country.

The Celtic Mystic, Singing Birds and Talking Trees

Ella Young was born in County Antrim in 1867. Her family moved to Dublin when she was very young, settling at first in Grosvenor Square, where one of her neighbours was George Russell (Æ). When she was older, she became one of Æ's protégées, known affectionately as the 'singing birds'. She was also an acquaintance of Padraig Pearse, with whom she shared a fervour for nationalism. In addition, Ella was a Celtic mythologist; her first book was entitled *Celtic Wonder Tales*, and she wrote poetry and children's tales inspired by Irish folklore. A member of Cumann na mBan, she served prison sentences for her Republican activities, including smuggling arms, but she felt the division of the Civil War keenly, and left Ireland for the USA in 1925. There, she lectured in Berkeley University, where her Celtic eccentricities were warmly embraced. Young remained in California until her death in 1956.

'We're Not Yahoos', said the Lord and Lady of Grosvenor Park

Husband and wife Edward Pakenham (1902–61) and Christine Pakenham (1900– 80) were prolific writers and patrons of Irish theatre. Also known as Lord and Lady Longford, they had a house in Grosvenor Park as well as their ancestral country pile in County Westmeath. They were initially involved with the Gate Theatre, but moved on to create their own group, the Longford Players, who performed many works written by Christine and Edward. Their most celebrated pieces were *Tankardstown* and *Yahoo* respectively, the latter of which was inspired by the life of Jonathan Swift. Christine Longford also made a name for herself as a novelist in the 1930s. These included *Making Conversation*, *Country Places*, *Jiggins of Jigginstown* and *Printed Cotton*.

Buried in Mount Jerome Cemetery, Lord Longford's headstone describes him as a poet and patriot. 'Happy and Sad Masks', the symbol of the theatre, are carved onto the sides of his headstone. The house was demolished in the 1970s and replaced with townhouses, bearing the same name, Grosvenor Park. He was also related to the founder of St Paul's Retreat, Mount Argus, Fr Paul Mary Pakenham.

From Charleville Road to the National Gallery

The father and son painters John B. Yeats (1839–1922) and Jack B. Yeats (1871–1957) lived at No. 14 Charleville Road in the 1880s. John B. Yeats became an even better known artist and portrait painter than his father and some of his works hang in the National Gallery of Ireland. All four of his children became important national and international cultural figures in early twentieth-century Ireland. One of these was the famous poet, W.B. Yeats. Another was a daughter, embroidery designer Susan

Mary (Lily), and yet another daughter of printing press fame (The Cuala Press) was Lolly Yeats.

Sherlock Chubby-Locks and a Fair Day in Mayo

Jack B. Yeats is widely regarded as Ireland's leading twentieth-century artist. In his early career, he earned money producing illustrations for magazines like *Boy's Own* and *Comic Cuts* (where he illustrated *Sherlock Chubby-Locks*). His paintings cover a diverse range of subject matter – everything from West of Ireland landscapes to circus performers – but all have a romantic, impressionistic style and raw emotional energy. He also tackled nationalism, Dublin, and the predicament of existence issues. One of his paintings, *A Fair Day, Mayo*, sold for one million euros in 2011, a record price in Ireland for art. Other famous works include *The Runaway Horse*.

Artist is Ireland's First Olympic Medallist

One of Jack B. Yeats' most famous paintings is *The Liffey Swim*, also on display in the National Gallery of Ireland. It helped create a most unusual record. It was thanks to this work that Yeats became Ireland's first Olympic medallist. He was awarded the silver medal in the arts and culture section of the 1924 Paris games. In the official papers of the games, Yeats' painting is recorded simply as 'Swimming'.

In 1957, he died at the Portobello Nursing Home at Portobello Bridge, overlooking the Grand Canal, and a short walk from Charleville Road. This is also where he created his final drawing.

One of Ireland's Most Gifted Impressionists – Walter F.

Walter Osborne was born on 17 June 1859 at No. 5 Castlewood Avenue, the second son of the painter William Osborne and his wife Anne Jane Woods. He was christened in Rathmines Church on 11 September of that year, after which point he appears to have mostly gone by his middle name, Frederick. Following in his father's footsteps, Frederick became an artist, and the general consensus is that he was Ireland's only true Impressionist. Upon finishing his schooling at C.W. Benson's school on Rathmines Road in 1876, he went to the RHA to study fine art, where he won two awards for his work.

Walter F. Osborne, RHA. *Pencil Sketch, by Nathaniel Hill; in the National Gallery of Ireland*

Osborne painted a wide variety of subjects. Portraits, landscapes and depictions of animals were lucrative, but his most resonant works are those that capture scenes of everyday nineteenth-century life. These humble scenes, which are imbued with a quiet dignity and a pervasive sense of admiration for the lives of ordinary people, won him acclaim. On a personal level, his character was likewise roundly admired.

Sadly, his illustrious career was to be a brief one. On 24 April 1903, Walter Frederick Osborne died of pneumonia in his home on Castlewood Avenue. He was 43. A Rathmines man until the last, he was buried in Mount Jerome Cemetery.

The Plough and the Stars and the Posh Lady

Sean O'Casey, in his famous play, *The Plough and the Stars*, has a minor character known as 'The Lady from Rathmines'. The play itself was named after the banner of the Irish Citizen Army. A cutting tragicomedy, the play satirises nationalistic idealism, which led to riots in Dublin upon its release. It is set in a tenement building during the Rising, where a distressed wife and expectant mother desperately tries to stop her idealistic husband from going to join his ICA comrades on the besieged streets. He disregards her pleas and is killed in the chaos, causing his wife to lose not only her unborn child, but her sanity.

Also in the play, a particular, 'Lady from Rathmines', with a posh accent, has got lost in Dublin city centre's tenement-land during the Rising. Moreover, she is fashionably dressed, stout and middle-aged for good measure! She meets some of the main characters in the play, including Fluther, Peter and The Covey. They are amused at her plight and her query. 'For Gawd's sake, will one of you kind men show any safe way for me to get to Wrathmines?'

13

SCHOOLS AND SCHOLARS

RATHMINES SCHOOL AND THE FAR EAST

The Soccer-playing Bishop and the Modernist Heretic

The Revd Dr Charles William Benson (1836–1919) opened his own school in 1858, when he was still only 21, at 48 Lower Rathmines Road. He remained there as headmaster for over forty years until 1899. As Church of Ireland priest Patrick Comerford explains on his comprehensive blog on Anglicanism, history, theology and more (patrickcomerford.com), 'The register of Benson's school reads like a potted social history of the Church of Ireland middle class in late Victorian Rathmines and Rathgar.' The school enrolled 2,190 boys; many went on to become top-class sportsmen, others served as missionaries around the world. Comerford goes on to provide an impressive sample of alumni:

> Other famous pupils included the artist Walter Osborne; the writer and painter George Russell, better known as 'AE'; the church historian Henry Patton, who was editor of the Church of Ireland Gazette before becoming Archdeacon and then Bishop of Killaloe; Henry Swanzy, who gave his name to Mount Swanzy, Canada; Newport White, Regius Professor of Divinity at TCD; Charles Osborne, biographer of the Portsmouth slum priest, Father Dolling; and George Tyrrell, who became a Catholic in 1879, went on to become a distinguished Jesuit, but fell foul of the Vatican for his 'modernist' theology.

Visitors to St Patrick's Cathedral can see a memorial to Benson in the south aisle. It was presented by former pupils. The inscription describes Rathmines School as 'one of the largest and most successful private schools in Ireland during the XIXth century'.

ST LOUIS HIGH SCHOOL –
THE FRENCH CONNECTION

Guaranteed Fresh Milk Daily!
St Louis High School on Charleville Road is an all-girls secondary school that was opened in 1913 to cater for the 'intellectual, spiritual, moral and emotional needs' of the daughters of middle-class Catholic families in the area. An unusual feature of St Louis school is the location of its Primary School – on Louis Lane just off Leinster Road, on one side, or via Williams Place behind the Swan Leisure Complex, just off the main Rathmines Road.

It all began when the Sisters of St Louis set up in Charleville House; on 1 September 1913 the school welcomed its first intake of thirty-six students. By the second term, the number had risen to eighty, and as the student population continued to grow over the next fifty years, the campus was constantly improved to make the environment more comfortable. A study of the history of the school on educationhistoryproject.wordpress.com, explains these improvements:

> Initially the only building was the main convent house, and from the start they had gas lighting. In 1914, they got a school cow for milk. Numbers grew to 240 students in 1921 when electric light was introduced. In 1929, the school was expanded with the purchase of an adjoining property, 8 Grosvenor Road, and then in 1942 the next-door property, 7 Grosvenor Road, was purchased. The concert hall and twelve extra classrooms were built in 1950. In 1965, a gym, a chapel and six more classrooms were added. The introduction of the Free Education Scheme in summer 1967 led to rapid expansion of enrolments. Further expansion continued up until 1982.

From France with a Flower of the Lily

The elegant crest of St Louis High school is full of symbolism. At first glance it looks quite simple, but every element has been considered to pay homage to the school's origins and namesake. The blue of the background is that of the Kings of France, St Louis, of course, having been King Louis IX, reigning from 1214 to 1279. The sword, with its crown of thorns, pays tribute to his time in the Crusades.

The fleur-de-lis on the bottom right is a famous French emblem, and a common feature of coats of arms. Opposite, there is a tower emblazoned with a red hand. This is taken from the crest of Monaghan town, where the Sisters of St Louis established their first school upon their arrival from France. The golden chain symbolises the bonds of charity, linking the Sisters and all those around the world with whom they work for the greater good. The school's pride in its heritage is also in evidence throughout the school, the crowning glory of which is the stained-glass window of St Louis in the chapel.

From Astrophysicist to The Forgotten Waltz – Famous Past Pupils

St Louis's list of alumni also has more than its fair share of impressive names. The school's history blog (educationhistoryproject.wordpress.com) shares a selection:

> Mary Black – singer; Joan Freeman – social activist; Finola O'Mahony – founder of Microsoft Ireland; Nessa O'Mahony – poet; Ita Daly – author; Anne Marie Madigan – astrophysicist; Siobhan McCarthy – Went End star; Aisling Cooney – Olympic swimmer and Anne Enright – author.

FROM A STABLE TO ST MARY'S

In 1890, the Holy Ghost Fathers bought Larkhill House (1841) and grounds on Rathmines Road, and thus began of one of Dublin's most famous and prestigious schools. Soon the stable and coach house were transformed into two classrooms, and an impressive assembly hall with a glass roof was built over the courtyard. During the works, the Fathers stayed at a rented house at No. 13 Leinster Square. On 9 September 1890 the school opened officially with about fifty pupils ranging from 9 to 17. This had doubled within a few months.

Lion-hearted Success on and off the Playing Fields

In 1896, *The Freeman's Journal* reported: 'The Holy Ghost Fathers have every reason to be proud. Because of the 754 Distinctions gained by all the colleges of Ireland their three schools, by themselves, have gained 160, which is more than one fifth of the whole; it is a truly phenomenal success!'

During 1934, the school was reorganised into Senior and Junior schools. It was during this period that sport really came to the fore for the school. The past pupils' Rugby Club had been relaunched in 1933 and many former students of St Mary's would go on to play for the Irish international team (including Sean Lynch, Ciaran Fitzgerald, John Moloney, Denis Hickie and Tony Ward). After the Second World War, the school acquired Kenilworth Square, and areas for rugby, cricket, tennis and basketball were all swiftly created to help nurture future talent.

Among other accomplishments in the second half of the twentieth century, the school opened a new 350-seat chapel in 1955, and in 1985, student Ronan McNulty won the titles of Irish and European Young Scientist of the Year.

A Patriot Place – Kevin Barry, Rory O'Connor and Dev

Eamon de Valera taught Maths in St Mary's from 1906 to 1910, and patriots Rory O'Connor and Kevin Barry were pupils of the school. Alongside patriots, sportspeople and influential figures in academia, government and business, well-known names in the St Mary's records include Jimmy O'Dea, Thomas J. Kiernan, and Seamus O'Braonáin. The future controversial archbishop of Dublin, John Charles McQuaid, was ordained in the chapel of St Mary's. Past pupils Tom and Ernest Farrell founded the Catholic Boy Scouts of Ireland in 1927.

Other notable alumni include RTÉ broadcaster Larry Gogan, Tom O'Higgins, former Chief Justice of the Supreme Court, a roll call of Ireland's rugby legends, and many more.

THE KILDARE PLACE SCHOOL

Banking on Coffee and Guinness

The Kildare Place Society has a school on Upper Rathmines Road. It was previously known as the Society for the Promotion of the Education of the Poor in Ireland. It was established at a location on Kildare Street by a group of businessmen (Bewley (coffee), Guinness (stout), La Touche (banking), etc., in 1811, its mission statement to improve standards of primary education throughout the country. Over the next two decades, the society established teacher training colleges and published in excess of one million schoolbooks. It lobbied for secular education, and this campaign would eventually lead to the foundation of the National School system in 1831. After this time, the society's funding was reallocated to the National Board, but it continued in operation, first as a Protestant education society and then as the Church of Ireland training college, which is now in Rathmines in the same complex as the school.

The original location of the Kildare Place School is now the site of the Department of Agriculture. The only reference to the first school is a street named School House Lane East, across the road from the Department. It moved to its present location adjacent to the Training College on Upper Rathmines Road in 1960.

14

STAGE, SCREEN AND THE RED-HEADED LADY

'DRINK, DRINK, DRINK TO EYES THAT ARE BRIGHT ...'

People associated with the theatre and film world and who had connections with Rathmines include Hollywood actress, Maureen O'Hara, and the world-famous film director, Rex Ingram. There is also Florence Stoker who took legal action against German film pirates over the film *Nosferatu*, the famous vampire film that had been made by her late husband. There were also the greats associated with the Abbey and Gate theatres including F.J. McCormick, the Fay Brothers and the Longfords, to name a few. Not only that, but one of Ireland's most famous musical societies, the Rathmines and Rathgar Musical Society

(affectionately known as the R & R) is still based in Rathmines more than 100 years after its founding. Moreover, two of Dublin's first cinemas, the Princess and the Stella, were located in Rathmines.

FROM THE PRINCESS TO CENSORSHIP

Interestingly, a former Rathmines resident, the author James Joyce, set up the first Irish cinema in 1909, called The Volta, located at Mary Street, Dublin. Four years later, in 1913, the Princess Cinema opened on Rathmines Road Lower. By the time another cinema, The Stella, opened in 1923 the township had been given supervision of cinemas in its area under the Censorship of Films Act, 1925. Three township censors had the task of passing or rejecting films shown in the area.

SISTER CINEMAS – MEMORIES OF 'THE PRINNER'

The Princess Cinema was one of the first purpose-built picture houses in the country when it opened in 1913. Known by all as 'The Prinner' it finally closed its doors on 2 July 1960. One man who has fond and very special memories of the Stella and her sister cinema further down the Rathmines Road, the Princess, is author George Kearns. George worked as an usher/doorman at the Princess and has written two books relating to Dublin cinemas including one called *The Prinner*. In a newspaper interview with *Dublin People*, he noted that 'The Princess, although not a blood relation, became a sister to the Stella when their directors decided to merge together the two most popular cinemas in the Rathmines area.' The Stella, facing Castlewood Avenue, closed more than forty years later.

WHEN THE TOWN HALL CLOCK STRUCK MIDNIGHT

Reflecting on the sad demise of the two regal and much attended cinemas, Mr Kearns said:

> The Princess, or 'Prinner' as most of her loyal subjects preferred to call her, took ill and closed on the night of July 2, 1960 as the Town Hall clock struck midnight and she never again played host to her patrons. She died in January of 1982 and her remains were laid to rest in a green field in Tallaght. Just like her sister, Stella took ill and closed her doors in the latter part of 2004 at the grand old age of 81 and for many years she rested and tried to regain her strength as her fans waited in vain for her recovery.

He continued with an air of hope. 'Fortunately, as a loyal doorman/usher to the beloved Princess, I have immortalised both her and her sister Stella forever,' he stated.

DUBLIN'S GOLDEN AGE OF CINEMA

The Stella was called after the wife of Anthony O'Grady, the owner of Slattery's Pub (originally called O'Grady's) and later owner of the Stella cinema itself. Generations of the O'Grady family ran the Stella for many years.

It was designed in a Classical style by the architectural firm Higginbotham & Stafford, and was described in a 1923 advertisement in The *Irish Times* as 'The largest, best ventilated, and most

luxuriously appointed cinema in Dublin'. The Stella Cinema opened in that great era, often described as 'the Golden Age of cinemas', spanning three decades from the 1920s. From the 1920s onwards, the Stella cinema became an integral part of the lives of Rathmines folk. Many cinemas from this period had additional functions, and echoing this trend the Stella Cinema also served as a public dance hall. The Stella was one of the oldest cinemas in Dublin when it closed in 2004.

ELVIS, THE BOOMTOWN RATS AND THE FLEA HOUSE

In addition to being a centre for the exhibition of film, the Stella was home to a number of cultural events during its history. The early silent film screenings were accompanied by a cinema orchestra, 'one of the best orchestras in Dublin' according to a 1923 *Irish Times* advertisement. The Stella was one of a proliferation of entertainment venues that burst onto the scene in the 1920s and '30s in response to a surge in popularity of film, music and dancing in the post-war years. These developments were not without detractors, but continued to thrive. The dance hall on the first floor was a very popular venue. It suffered a decline in the 1940s but continued to be used as a venue for dance lessons. Several music gigs were held in the Stella Cinema in the 1970s, including the Boomtown Rats (December 1977) and Elvis Costello (March 1978).

In its later years, many locals referred to the Stella as 'the flea pit' or 'flea house' ('you'd go in crippled and come out walking/running').

STELLA AND THE SURVIVAL OF THE FITTEST

It has been quite an extraordinary feat on the part of owners, conservationists and architects to resurrect this extraordinary cinema, full as it is of architectural gems and history. Now called the Stella Theatre, but always known just as 'the Stella', the cinema's re-birth and recovery from 2017 onwards was truly an adventure. In that year it was decided by the new owners, the Press Up Entertainment Group (acquired from the Ward

Anderson Group, Ireland's largest cinema chain), to re-open the cinema in all its former glory. They had not anticipated, however, that which had been hidden under grime, dust, and old plasterwork and partitions for decades. For there they discovered the original structural and decorative features of the historic building in all their architectural glory, having survived virtually intact since 1923. Whether it was at the entrance, the auditorium, the banisters and steps on the curved staircase, mosaic floors, carved figurines and the decorative arch surrounding the original screen, all were re-discovered.

With much fanfare, including the attendance of An Taoiseach, Leo Varadkar, the cinema was finally opened in late 2018. Since then it has regained also its enormous popularity with happy patrons enjoying the ambience and luxury of yesteryear. Right next door to the cinema, the owners have converted a former banking hall into a restaurant, named 'The Diner', in honour of the unknown diner who regularly frequented the original cinema.

THE ABBEY THEATRE TRIANGLE – FAY, BLYTHE AND MCCORMICK

Just off Palmerston Road is Ormond Road and at No. 12 lived the famous Fay Brothers, Frank and Willie, stage directors and actors who were much involved in the establishment of the Abbey Theatre. They founded an acting group called the Ormond Dramatic Company (1891) later the Ormond Players, named after their road, and this group staged George Russell's *Deirdre* and W.B. Yeats's *Kathleen Ni Houlihan* in St Teresa's Hall, Clarendon Street. Yeats once declared that the national theatre owed its existence to the two Fay brothers. It was they who established the W.G. Fay's National Dramatic Company in 1902 that focused on developing Irish acting talent, that staged Russell's and Yeats' plays, and that subsequently led to the foundation of the Abbey Theatre. And it was also the Fays who found the site, the Mechanic's Institute Hall on Abbey Street, that became the site for the national theatre. Two years later in 1904 it opened its doors for the first time.

THE ABBEY PLAYERS IN THEIR CELTIC ROLES AT THE HARRIS

Upper row (left to right)—Denis O'Dea and Aideen O'Connor Arthur Shields and Eileen Crowe, F. J. McCormick and May Craig At bottom—Barry Fitzgerald and Fiona Wallace

F.J. McCormick was a member of the Abbey Players and lived at Palmerston Road, Rathmines.

FROM IRISH VOLUNTEER TO ABBEY DIRECTOR

Ernest Blythe (1885–1975), for many years the Director of the Abbey Theatre, lived at No. 6 Temple Villas, around the corner from Ormond Road. He later lived at 50 Kenilworth Square until his death in 1975. Ernest Blythe, TD and later Senator, successively Minister for Finance, Post & Telegraphs, and Trade & Commerce. Blythe was born in Co. Antrim, where he was a government clerk and reporter with the *North Down Herald*. He was an unusual figure in Ireland's fight for independence, being a Protestant Unionist. Blythe was a member of Conradh na Gaeilge, the IRB and was an Irish Volunteer organiser. In the historic elections of 1918 that saw the old Irish Parliamentary Party heavily defeated, Blythe was elected a Sinn Féin TD for Monaghan. He was later was Minister for Finance in the Free State Government in 1923 and then Vice-President of the Executive Council (deputy head of government). From 1941 to 1967 he was managing director of the Abbey Theatre and remained a director until 1972.

THE ACTORS' STRIKE AND
THE ODD MAN OUT

Blythe grant-aided the theatre, making it the first state-subsidised theatre in the world, but he was no stranger to opposition. Many disapproved of his fondness for comedies and works featuring ordinary scenarios. He was interested in making money, but also in the democratisation of theatre, which was roundly criticised by those who favoured more high-brow drama. He did champion emerging playwrights who would go on to be giants of Irish theatre, including Brian Friel and Hugh Leonard, but tensions remained. Respected actor and director Vincent Dowling led an actors' strike against him and in 1967 he resigned as Managing Director, just before the opening of the new theatre. Blythe was a divisive figure until the end; while he considered himself to be a very practical nationalist, there were those who considered him to be something of a communist troublemaker.

TO BE VERSATILE OR NOT VERSATILE
– THAT WAS THE QUESTION

One of the Abbey's most celebrated actors, F.J. McCormick (1899-1947) lived at No. 16 Palmerston Gardens. The dramatist Lennox Robinson said that McCormick was the 'most versatile' of Abbey actors but his relationship with Séan O'Casey was not so amiable; after a performance of *The Plough and the Stars* the actor turned to the audience and said, 'Don't blame the actors. We didn't write the play.' McCormick's success was not limited to the Dublin stage, however. He also had a healthy film career during the 1940s and '50s. He featured in the 1947 film *Hungry Hill* and was singled out for praise in the *New York Times*' review: 'As the butler who served John Brodrick, his sons, and their sons in turn, the late F.J. McCormick is truly magnificent, giving an even more subtle portrayal of Irish character than he did as the wily tramp in *Odd Man Out*.'

THE LORD AND THE COUNTESS – THE LONGFORDS OF THE GATE THEATRE

Edward Arthur Henry Pakenham, 6th Earl of Longford (1902–61), was a theatre patron, playwright, translator and Irish politician (being a member of Seanad Éireann in the late 1940s) who is best remembered as a former Director of the renowned Gate Theatre in Dublin. The family lived on Leinster Road (Grosvenor Park) during the week and in Pakenham Hall (now Tullynally Castle), Longford, at the weekends. Edward and Christine (the Countess of Longford) founded Longford Productions in 1936. The Gate was founded by Micheál MacLiammóir and Hilton Edwards in 1928, but by 1931 it had already run into financial difficulties. Lord Longford offered to buy the outstanding shares, which was a divisive suggestion that led to five years of tense arguments and negotiation. In the end, the company was split into Edwards-MacLiammóir Productions and Longford Productions, with each group entitled to six months in the theatre (the other six to be spent touring). Longford Productions enjoyed a productive twenty-four years of operation, staging 151 plays at the Gate and performing for countless thrilled audiences nationwide.

'TIS HERSELF' – THE FAMOUS REDHEADED HOLLYWOOD ACTRESS

The Bernadette Players
In the shadow of the fine church and along Richmond Hill was, for many years, the home of the Bernadette Players, an amateur drama/musical society that used

Sketch of Hollywood actors Maureen O'Hara and John Wayne. Maureen had received her early training with the Bernadette Players at Richmond Hill.

to meet in Bernadette Hall. This was where Maureen O'Hara, Donal Donnelly, Christopher Cassin, Brendan McShane and other luminaries started their illustrious careers. The old building is now gone, having been replaced by a small block of apartments, also called Bernadette Hall.

From Rathmines Theatre Company to Mayflower Pictures

Maureen O'Hara (1920–2015), the legendary Hollywood actress, had Rathmines connections – this is where her illustrious career started. The flame-haired O'Hara specialised in feisty, passionate heroines, and her most cherished role remains the wonderful Mary Kate Danaher in *The Quiet Man*, on which she worked with her frequent collaborators, John Wayne and director John Ford.

The O'Hara family lived on Beechwood Avenue Upper in Ranelagh, but the young Maureen spent a lot of time in Rathmines. An early performer, she attended classes for singing, dancing, drama and elocution, and at the age of 10 she joined the Rathmines Theatre Company. She was also with the Bernadette Players at Richmond Hill. She began winning amateur acting competitions and Feis events, and by 13 was hired to perform classical plays on Radio Éireann. Maureen joined the Abbey Theatre in 1934 and set about working her way up from the very bottom; she was cast in her first lead role three years later. Before she made her debut, however, she was spotted by American singer Harry Richman, who whisked her off to London to meet with Charles Laughton. Without hesitation, Laughton snapped her up for Mayflower Pictures with a seven-year contract. The rest, as they say, is history. O'Hara's film career was extraordinary, as she more than held her own against Hollywood's greatest leading men, including Errol Flynn, James Stewart and Henry Fonda.

On Wings of an Eagle to Hollywood

Maureen O'Hara is nothing short of a Hollywood icon. In a Golden Age of cinema, with stiff competition from numerous starlets and bombshells, she was thought to be one of the most beautiful women in the world. She had the acting talent to match, of course, and her incendiary chemistry with the great John Wayne produced five of her best-remembered performances, in *Rio Grande* (1950), *The Quiet Man* (1952), *The Wings of Eagles* (1957), *McLintock!* (1963) and *Big Jake* (1971). Maureen had homes in Arizona, the Virgin Islands and lived mainly in Glengarriff, County Cork, after suffering a stroke in 2005. She died in 2015 at the age of 95.

Rebel at Heart – the Great Film Director
Film-maker Rex Ingram was born Reginald Ingram Montgomery Hitchcock at No. 58 Grosvenor Square in 1892. His father was a Church of Ireland minister, and so Rex's childhood years were spent moving from parish to parish. It was perhaps this unsettled existence that led to his idiosyncratic, defiant nature. A schoolfriend named R.D. Greer, quoted in a Trinity College biography, described him as follows:

> A rebel at heart he had a discomforting disdain for authority, and escapades brought him into close conflict with those responsible for discipline. But Rex was never at a loss, and actually on one occasion challenged a master 'to lay down his master's robes and come out behind the "gym" and see who is the better man'.

Whether due to his rejection by Trinity or his natural restlessness in the face of the limitations of a small country, Rex left Ireland for good in 1911.

Rex Ingram, film director and master of the silent film era, lived at Grosvenor Square, Rathmines.

The Four Horsemen of the Apocalypse

Ingram studied sculpture at the Yale University School of Art, but he quickly found his calling in film. He began acting in 1913, before moving behind the camera. He was interested in writing, production and directing, and he had his first producer-director credit on *The Great Problem* in 1916. After a spell in a number of top studios, he signed with Metro in 1920. He was taken under the wing of the trailblazing screenwriter June Mathis, and together they made four films: *Hearts are Trump* (1920), *The Four Horsemen of the Apocalypse* (1921), *The Conquering Power* (1921), and *Turn to the Right* (1922).

The Walk of Fame and The Red Shoes

Ingram married twice, first to actress Doris Pawn in 1917 and later to Alice Terry, whom he was with from 1921 until his death. In 1925, he co-directed the classic epic *Ben Hur* with Fred Niblo. Part of the move was filmed in Italy, and it was during this period that Rex and Alice decided to relocate to the French Riviera. They established a film studio in Nice and filmed a great deal on location throughout Southern Europe for Hollywood studios. One of Ingram's employees there was Michael Powell, who himself would go on to direct a classic – *The Red Shoes* (1948). Powell co-directed with Emeric Pressburger, but Ingram's surrealist influence looms large on screen.

Ingram's films were highly respected by his contemporaries, who considered him a bold visionary. In 1949 he was named an honorary life member of the Directors' Guild of America. He died on 21 July 1950, aged 58, but his star on the Hollywood Walk of Fame can still be visited at 1651 Vine Street, Los Angeles.

When Oscar Wilde's Girlfriend Met Bram Stoker

Rathmines resident Florence Balcombe (17 July 1858–25 May 1937) married Bram Stoker in Dublin in 1878. Prior to her marriage, the noted beauty lived at No. 66 Palmerston Road and she was courted by Oscar Wilde, who had been friends with Stoker since Trinity. Wilde was said to be bereft when Florence chose his friend, but they later reconciled, with Stoker even visiting him in exile. The Stokers settled in London, where Bram managed Henry Irving's Lyceum Theatre for some twenty-seven years. Their only child, Irving Noel Thornley Stoker, was born in 1879.

The Clash of Nosferatu and Dracula

Upon Stoker's death in 1912, Florence became the literary executor of his work, and she was responsible for the eradication of the (now classic) 1922 horror film *Nosferatu*. The movie was very clearly based on Dracula, but the makers neither credited the source nor cleared the required permission to adapt the tale. Balcombe received an anonymous letter from Berlin alerting her to the piece, and she was justly enraged. She was a struggling widow, and here was a company profiting from the work that she controlled. She immediately demanded remuneration and the destruction of all prints and negatives of the film.

THE RATHMINES AND RATHGAR MUSICAL SOCIETY

Rathmines and Rathgar Musical Society.

FIRST SEASON · 1913 - 1914.

CONCERT

TOWN HALL, RATHMINES.

22nd April, 1914.
Book of Words.

In the area of music, Dublin has always been a musical city and had many musical societies in the early decades of the twentieth century. It also had music halls such as the Empire Palace and the Tivoli, the Antient Concert Rooms and the Theatre Royal with seating for nearly 2,500 people. The present-day Olympia Theatre was originally Dan Lowry's Music Hall. The Gaiety Theatre opened in 1872 and became famous for its annual pantomime.

The R & R and High-Class Musicals

One of the most famous musical societies, and still going strong, is the Rathgar and Rathmines Musical Society. The R & R, as it is affectionately known, has been in continuous operation since it was founded in 1913. This is a singular achievement. A history of the R & R, on the society's website, explains:

[The R & R is] the only musical society in continuous existence, producing two, maybe three shows a year in the principal theatres of Dublin and the National Concert Hall without interruption since 1913. With over 100 years under its belt, the R & R has produced over 250 shows with approximately 2,600 performances. It all started in 1913 at a meeting held in 48 Summerville Park, Rathmines, nearly across the road from the present-day site of the R & R's premises. C.P. Fitzgerald, who was the young organist at that time in Rathgar's Church of the Three Patrons, wanted to establish a musical society whose membership would be formed from residents of the Township of Rathmines and Rathgar.

He persuaded a group of friends into forming a musical society, and, as they all lived in Rathgar or Rathmines, the Society was christened accordingly. Fitzgerald was the conductor. Edwin Lloyd, a solicitor from Kenilworth Square, was Chairman, W.G. Mulvin of York Road was Honorary Secretary and J.C. O'Brien of Belgrave Square, the Producer. The controversial businessman William Martin Murphy of Dartry Hall became President. The objectives of the proposed musical society were the study of, and production of, operatic, choral and other high-class musical works. By the end of 1913, the Society was sufficiently organised to book the Gaiety Theatre for December and to produce Gilbert & Sullivan's *The Mikado*. Notwithstanding the passing of the years and even into the twenty-first century, the society remains faithful to its original objective.

From the Yeoman of the Guard to the Feis Ceoil

In December of the following year, the society brought Gilbert & Sullivan to the grand Gaiety Theatre for the first time, this time performing *Yeomen of the Guard*. A staging of Planquette's *Les Cloches de Corneville* in 1915 inspired the society to broaden its scope, to give its all of its members as many opportunities as possible to showcase their various talents.

For over a century, the R & R has played a significant role in Dublin's music and theatre scenes, and it has also enjoyed an amiable relationship with the Feis Ceoil. In 1946, the society present the Feis with a cup that was to be awarded for the best performance of a light opera piece.

Famous members who went on to the professional and other stages – include Frank Fay and Ria Mooney (Abbey Theatre), David Kelly, Jack Mac Gowran, T.P McKenna and Terry Wogan.

Buried but Very Much Alive!

There are some more interesting facts about the R & R, and it is worth visiting their website (randr.ie) to read about the often surprising characters who trod the boards with the society. Count Casimir Markievicz, husband of Constance Gore-Booth, for example, took part in *Yeomen of the Guard* during the 1914 Gaiety Theatre debut. The R & R made its way into classic fiction when it was mentioned in *At Swim Two Birds* by Flann

O'Brien in 1939, and in 1998, Brian Hayes TD appeared in the 1998 production of *Fiddler on the Roof*.

When then Lord Mayor of Dublin Seán Haughey buried a time capsule on North Earl Street in 1989, its artefacts included the R & R 75th anniversary record and other ephemera celebrating the society's achievements and its close links with the city's cultural life.

Start Spreading the News!

Rathmines is a hive of activity and the Rathmines Amateur Dramatic Society is part of that. This talented society, also known as RADS, was formed in the summer of 2011 by a group of drama enthusiasts in the Rathmines area. Most had undertaken drama courses in Rathmines College. Their first production was *Spreading the News*, set in the West of Ireland, and was shown in December 2011 in the Lower Deck at Portobello Bridge.

15

PARKS, SPORTS AND THE GREAT OUTDOORS

TRANQUILLA AND BELGRAVE PARKS

Tranquilla Park (a.k.a. the Spotty Tunnel Park with very small children), a small park with a children's playground and some sporting facilities, is located on the site of the former grounds of the Tranquilla Convent on Rathmines Road Upper. The convent was founded by the Carmelite Sisters in 1833, who remained here until the 1970s. The only reminder today of that enclosed order of nuns is the Tranquilla Lodge beside the park. On the old wall of the former convent, now topped with park railings, near the park's entrance, and opposite Rathmines Close, is a faded and barely visible plaque to Tomás O'Laoghaire, a young man from Armstrong Street in Harold's Cross, who, according to the inscription, was murdered on 23 March 1923 during the Irish Civil War.

Belgrave Square Park is located in the calm and leafy surroundings of the square of the same name. It, too, caters for children of all ages.

FROM BATTLES WITH CROMWELL TO BATTLES WITH CHILDREN – PALMERSTON PARK

During the English Civil War, one of the most decisive battles in the history of Ireland took place in 1649 – the Battle of Rathmines. Some of the fighting took place at what is now the south side of Palmerston Park. Today, it is the site of a fine secluded park and children's playground.

In 1746, Henry 1st Viscount Palmerston came into possession of the surrounding lands, and the grounds were offered to the Rathmines Township Commissioners in 1881. Lord Palmerston's agents stipulated that the land was to be used as a public park, and that the deal would see several of the roads therein fall under the responsibility of the commissioners. After a period of negotiation, they came to an agreement, and in 1893 the park was created by William Sheppard, who was, at that time, the most renowned landscape architect in the country. Sheppard was at the top of his game in the three decades between 1880 and the First World War. He died in 1933 and is buried in Mount Jerome Cemetery. In the north choir aisle of St Patrick's Cathedral, you can see a grand stained-glass window that Sheppard commissioned in memory of his wife.

THE SPORTING LIFE

The Leinster Cricket Club and W.C. Fields
Leinster Cricket Club is one of the oldest in the world. Founded in 1852, it was originally located on Observatory Lane before moving to its current location in 1865. The club has been the scene of numerous historic occasions. It played host to the famous W.C. Fields and his brother G.F. Fields in 1874 – the last time that the two brothers hit centuries in the same game. In addition, Irish Rugby Union had its first home game here, in 1875. Today, the grounds, including the cricket club, are known as Leinster Sports Complex.

The Lambert Connection and the LCC
Many associated with the Leinster Cricket Club on Observatory Lane will have fond memories of epic games fought. The late Martin D. Burke, the club's longest serving captain up until his 96th year, was an outstanding member of the all-conquering LCC sides of the 1930s, '40s and early '50s. He was one of an elite group to have scored over 500 runs in a season. Another

name also stands out, that of Bob Lambert. It was a big occasion, the presentation of the Marchant Cup of 1921. This 1985 article from the archives of *Cricket Leinster* tells the tale:

> His Honour Judge Green, president of the Leinster Cricket Union, expressed his 'unbounded gratification that, after 30 years of strenuous cricket, his old friend was as virile and active as ever, and still the mainstay of the international XI'. As Robert Hamilton Lambert moved to the platform to receive the trophy, tremendous applause welled up from the huge gathering, many of whom, now retired, had once played with and against the Great Man. Handing over the trophy, his Honour commented: 'Lambert's extraordinary batting average of 217 is a feat few will be capable of rivalling.'

A Colossus and Titan of Sport

Considered a 'titan among batsmen' and regularly cited as Ireland's greatest ever cricketer, Bob Lambert was just 15 years old when he debuted for the Leinster Senior Team. Within two years he had won a place on the Ireland team, which he would go on to captain for three decades. One newspaper reported:

> A hit which will live in memory was that made by Bob against County Kildare as far back as 1904. These were the days when the Short Grass county could put a really strong team in the field. W.H. Harrington and W. Keyes were then at their best, and Lambert hit Harrington onto the roof of a house on the far side of Mountpleasant Avenue - a hit never claimed before or since.

Bob Lambert will forever be a hero of Irish cricket. According to a piece commemorating his prowess in the Cricket Ireland Archives, 'Asked by a cricket correspondent if Lambert would have been an even greater cricketer had he played regularly in England, W.G. Grace replied: "How do you improve on perfection?"'

Lambert, the LCC and Ulysses!
Indeed, respect for Lambert's skills extended well beyond the cricket pavilion. James Joyce was so impressed with his unique and skilful style of batting that he mentioned him in *Ulysses*.

ST MARY'S RUGBY CLUB – STRENGTH AT ALL TIMES

Lions and Legends of Rugby
Since its very early years, St Mary's College has been associated with top-quality rugby. It remains the major sport of the college on Rathmines Road, their colours blue and white often brightening the area around the school. Its motto is 'Fidelitas in Arduis' – 'Strong in Difficult Times'. The renowned club has produced over thirty schools international players since 1975 – more than almost any other school – as well as several international players including Denis Hickie, Tony Ward, Jonathan Sexton, Sean Lynch and Seamus Deering. The school is considered one of the top rugby-playing schools in Leinster.

Old St Mary's and Side-Stepping the Dung
St Mary's College RFC was formed at St Mary's College in September 1900. Originally known as Old Mary's FC, its ethos was to be an 'open club, playing open rugby', a tradition of which its members remain fiercely proud. In the early days, the matches were played in the front field at the college and the first trophy, the Leinster Junior Cup, was won in 1905. For many years they trained at Kimmage Grove, near Harold's Cross, on a field rented from a local farmer. Despite the obvious challenges of playing on agricultural land, this was a happy era for the club; they won numerous junior cups, and, in dodging sheep and cattle dung, they developed 'the best side-steps in Dublin rugby' (stmaryscollegerfc.com).

Winning the Most Prestigious Trophy
In 1955, the club moved to new grounds on College Drive, off Fortfield Road. These excellent new facilities ushered in a

golden age for St Mary's. As quickly as 1957/8, the club brought home its first Leinster Senior Cup, under the captaincy of Joe Fanagan and with wonderful players like Ned Carmody, Vincent Mc Govern, Sean Cooke, Jack Bagnall, the Hussey twins, Dick Whitty, Ken Wall and Nicky Corrigan. The LSC at that time was the most prestigious trophy and the most difficult to win in Irish rugby.

The Glorious Age – From Triple Crowns to Lions

During the 1960s, St Mary's juniors won a wealth of silverware, and in 1969 Sean Lynch led his team to senior victory once again (Lynch then became the club's first international and first British and Irish Lion). Always building upon their strength, status and experience, the club won the cup again in 1971, '74, '75,'87, '93, '95, 2005 and 2010. St Mary's won the IRFU centenary All-Ireland Cup, led by the wonderful Johnny Moloney in 1975.

As the club's website affirms, the 1970s were the 'glorious age':

> with many trophies at all levels being won and with outstanding players including Sean Lynch, Dennis Hickie, John Moloney, Tom Grace, Seamus Deering, Tom Feighery, Tony Ward, Terry Kennedy, Ciaran Fitzgerald and Rodney O'Donnell, all being capped for Ireland. Of course, Johnny Moloney, Tom Grace and super-hero Seamus Deering captained Ireland during that period, and later Ciaran Fitzgerald captained Ireland to a Triple Crown in '82 and '85 and captained the Lions in 1983.

Today, the club can boast ten Lions, twenty-six full internationals, three club internationals, over 120 inter-provincial players stretching back to 1911, several A inter-provincial, A international, Underage international and Colleges international players. St Mary's College RFC has won over 100 LB/IRFU trophies. The legend continues!

THE OLDEST BOWLING CLUB IN IRELAND

The oldest lawn bowling club in the Republic of Ireland, the Kenilworth Bowling Club, which is on Grosvenor Square, was founded in 1892. It is also the only club in the Republic with two bowling greens, one artificial and one grass. The Kenilworth Bowling Club has a very interesting history, being associated with the Easons family of bookshop fame.

Bowls as we know it today found its form in the late 1800s, but the game had been played in Dublin for centuries prior, both on public and private greens. Indeed, the origins of the Marlborough Street gardens can be traced back to a twelfth-century bowling green.

Exercising after the Fatigues of Study

In Dublin, the oldest bowling green was on Hoggen Green, which contained College Green. A piece from the annals of the Bowling League of Ireland (irishlawnbowls.ie) explains:

> Over three centuries ago the city authorities made an order that 'Robert Taylor should be allowed to make what profit and benefit he can of the free use and exercise of bowling, and that he shall have charge and care of looking after and overseeing the said unrailed bowling place in Hoggen Green during our pleasure.' There is also a record of a bowling green in Trinity College, 'for the exercise of the students after the fatigues of their studies'.

There was another green in Chapelizod, which was run by the Victoria Bowling Club. Play here was restricted to Tuesdays and Fridays, and members were offered transportation from Essex Quay.

The Earl, the Honourable, the Lord and the Chief Secretary

There is no record of bowls being played in the early nineteenth century, but in 1892 a bowling club was formed in Rathmines that is still thriving to this day. As relayed by the Bowling League of Ireland, a group of 'influential "upper class" gentlemen' met at either No. 29 or No. 30 Kenilworth Square (both were owned by Charles Eason, well-known bookseller) and formed Kenilworth Bowling Club. The first members were similarly affluent – mostly businessmen, many of them English and Scottish – and the first woods were rolled on the rear lawn of Eason's property.

Books, Bowls and Balls

In those days the club played at Kenilworth Square, and there can be little doubt as to the social standing of its membership. The early patrons were the Lord Lieutenant, the Earl of Aberdeen, and the Honourable H.W. Long, the Chief Secretary. In 1906 the club held its first Annual Ball in Rathmines Town Hall. This would have been a chic affair, judging by the price of the tickets; single tickets were 10s and doubles, 15s – hardly small change in those days!

Laws of the Game – 'Not Quite Bowls, Old Chap!'

While Kenilworth Square was sufficient for the club's requirements initially, the ground suffered during the winter, when it was used for football and other less genteel sports, leaving it far from ideal for bowls. In 1909, a limited company was formed and land leased at nearby Grosvenor Square. A proper bowling green was laid and later, in 1922, the freehold was purchased for £485.

The original founding member clubs of the Bowling League of Ireland were Kenilworth (established 1892), Railway Union (1904), Blackrock (1906), Leinster (1913) and Clontarf (1925). The league was conceived on 25 March 1927, when a Mr W. Clarke invited these clubs to a meeting, at which it was proposed that an association would be a tremendous asset that would allow them to control the game in the Republic.

Stratford Lawn Tennis Club and Mr Irish Tennis

Stratford Lawn Tennis Club shares the Grosvenor Square grounds with Kenilworth. One former member during the 1960s stands out in particular. Alf Walsh was 'Mr Irish Tennis' and is remembered as the sport's greatest ambassador here. He ran the Irish Lawn Tennis Association from his Leinster Road kitchen, a stone's throw from the club. Tennis Ireland remembers him as a particular champion for small, provincial clubs and for smaller tennis-playing countries. Tennis Ireland explains how he had his concerns about the advent of open tennis:

> [It] was initially a cause for concern to Walsh, who greatly valued Ireland's position of relative authority in the international administration of the game. However, once it became clear that professional tennis was the future of the game, Walsh graciously accepted and embraced the new system so as to achieve the maximum benefits for Irish clubs and players. Sociable, charming and boundlessly energetic, Alf Walsh was a wonderful ambassador for Irish tennis and one of life's true gentlemen.

Other tennis clubs in the Rathmines vicinity are the Brookfield (dating from 1906) at Palmerston Park, and the Ashbrook, off Grosvenor Road, which has been in existence since 1922. Both have interesting histories.

16

THE STEAMBOAT LADIES AND THE DROPPING WELL

IS IT DARTRY OR IS IT RATHMINES?

Dartry Road begins at the junction of Upper Rathmines Road, Highfield Road and Palmerston Park and continues just beyond the former Dartry Dye works, following the course of the River Dodder down to the famous Dropping Well pub. This road, while part of the separate area of Dartry, is intrinsically linked with Rathmines and Rathgar and residents of both areas sometimes claim to be part of the other area. The confusion was possibly caused since Dartry Road once began in the vicinity of No. 215 Upper Rathmines Road where there is a plaque embedded into the wall, on the upper front elevation of the house, that reads: 'Fitzwilliam Terrace, Lr Dartry Road, Upr Rathmines, 1905'. So, are we to say then that Upper Rathmines Road is really Lower Dartry Road? Or is Lower Dartry really Rathmines?

Houses on Dartry Road itself date from c.1840 with St Kevin's House at No. 21c, built in 1849. Cora Linn at No. 2 was built in 1874, and nearby Santon dates from 1877. Dartry House, off Orwell Woods, dates from 1810.

STEAMBOATS, TRINITY AND DANGERS TO MEN

Located along Dartry Road, facing the older three- and four-storey red-bricked houses of Sunbury Gardens, is Trinity Hall, the most important residence for students of Trinity College Dublin (TCD). There are three detached Victorian mansions in the grounds of Trinity Hall that are surrounded by very modern red-bricked halls of residence.

Women were admitted as students of TCD in 1904 but were regarded by the authorities as 'a danger to men'. Consequently, in 1908, the college purchased a house called 'Glen-na- Smoil' in order to create a hall of residence for women. The house, later renamed Oldham, stood on the grounds where the current Trinity Hall is located. It had to be in a 'nice' suburb, as near as possible to the college but far enough away not to distract the male students on campus. It was imperative that they were not a danger to the men.

LORD IVEAGH AND THE CAMPAIGNING ELIZABETH OLDHAM

A great deal of the funds raised came from donations from Lord Iveagh, the university's chancellor, Frederick Purser, a senior fellow, and fees paid by female Oxford and Cambridge students. Sometimes referred to as 'steamboat ladies' due to their choice of transport to Dublin, these women paid for the conferral of University

Poster, 2017, showing Rathmines Garden Trail.

of Dublin degrees under a system that existed between these institutions. In its early years, the hall welcomed more than 700 of these students. In 1910, the site was extended thanks to the donation of Palmerston House and grounds by John Griffith. Griffith was a relative of Frederick Purser, and so the building was renamed Purser House in his honour.

Oldham House was the primary residence for ladies of the college until the early 1970s. The two other buildings are called Purser and Greenane houses. It is a fine detached Victorian building named after Elizabeth Oldham, one of the main campaigners for women's admission to the college. Her portrait hangs in the front lounge. The hall continued as a residence for females until the 1970s, when the first men were admitted.

RATHMINES GARDEN TRAIL AND THE EXOTIC BOTANIC GARDENS

It was only when one participated in the Rathmines Garden Trail that the hidden gem that is the Trinity College Botanic Gardens was discovered. Located in the grounds of Trinity Hall, and running parallel to Palmerston Park, the garden has been located here since 1968.

The Botanic Gardens, connected to the Botany Department in Trinity, moved to a site in Trinity Hall when the lease on the original site in Ballsbridge (where the two hotels were built on the corner of Lansdowne Road) was bought back – hence some of the slightly more exotic trees in the area. There were vegetable plots there which continued to supply the Hall for meals, and one of the arrangements was that a fresh vase of flowers would be picked and placed in the hall of Main House each week. The gardens gradually turned more and more to experimental growing, and some of the area which was mostly orchard was used in the new build a decade ago.

Lucy the Cat and the Giant Golden Irises

Despite that, the gardens boast some 1,000 species of plants and more than 100 varieties of shrubs and trees. A plant with the striking name of *Crocosmia Lucifer* is patrolled regularly by a black cat, appropriately called Lucy. The name derives from deep red colour of the flowers that are like giant Golden Irises. There are also ponds, beehives and glasshouses in this haven of tranquillity which even boasts its own micro-climate.

The gardens are also part of the annual Rathmines Garden Trail that starts with the Botanic Gardens and continues to 11 Bessborough Parade, 137 Leinster Road, 149 Leinster Road, 27 Leinster Square, 29 Leinster Square, 6 Prince Arthur Terrace and ending at Mount Anthony on Ardee Road, just off the main Rathmines Road.

DARTRY DYE WORKS – WASHING THE QUEEN'S LAUNDRY

There were a number of mills built along the River Dodder in the eighteenth and nineteenth centuries. Dartry Limited was established in 1888 as the Dublin Laundry Company, with its works beside the Nine Arches Bridge (that magnificent viaduct that now carries the LUAS) and the River Dodder at Dartry. All that remains of the mill is the free-standing towering chimney that used to be part of the works. According to Dublin City Public Libraries, in 1900 the laundry claimed to be the second largest in the United Kingdom and Ireland, and the official launderer to Queen Victoria when she visited Ireland.

In 1895, an old mill near where the Dartry Road slopes down to the Dodder was converted into the Dartry Dye Works, and the red-bricked building, known as the Counting House, was added in the 1920s. In 1955, the two businesses (the laundry and the dye works) amalgamated, with the name The Dublin Laundry and Dartry Dye Works. It ceased business in 1983 as more homes had washing machines and had no need for laundries. Not too long afterwards, another laundry that catered for the houses of Rathmines, the Kelso Laundry on Lower Rathmines Road, also closed.

THE COUNTING HOUSE AND THE STOPPED CLOCK

Today, the Counting House of Dartry Dye Works is still standing, though now in offices. The figures 'Est. 1895' are carved below the still-working clock and above the stained-glass windows. Under the windows, the words 'Dartry Dye Works' are still emblazoned over the old front entrance of this fine red-bricked building. The clock, which is now digitalised, is so popular with passers-by that when it stopped a number of years ago, the public were so disconcerted that many wrote to the owners requesting that it be fixed post-haste! The adjacent buildings, Dartry Mills, were demolished, and new offices were built, though retaining the old name. A very steep and winding road hurtles down to Dodder Park – a joy for many a downward cyclist!

THE GREAT FAMINE AND THE DROPPING WELL

The Mortuary and the Granite Bridge
Just down the hill from the Dartry Dye Works, and with the bridge of nine arches in view, is the landmark Dropping Well pub by the riverside. It was built in 1847 on the site of a mortuary that was created to help address the tragic problem of bodies being washed along in the River Dodder. It was common at that time for the destitute to convene along its banks, with many succumbing to their extreme hunger, and when John Howe and his wife applied for a liquor licence, their main motivation was to give these people some dignity in death.

Later, the Dropping Well became a popular escape for thirsty pilgrims who would walk the 3 miles from Dublin city centre to avoid the 'Holy Hour' (2.30–3.30 P.M.), when all the pubs there were closed.

In the late eighteenth century, Milltown was a bustling area, full of trade, with corn, iron and paper mills, and a strong silk industry. There was also a sawmill, which was located close to the site of the Dropping Well, at what is now known as Classon's Bridge. John Classon's milling business was here and he had the bridge built, using granite from the river bed, to allow for more efficient incoming and outgoing traffic at the mill.

Black '47 and the Huddled Masses of Famine Victims in Dublin

The Dropping Well was born of the Great Famine of 1845 to 1849. It was during the worst year of the disaster, known as Black '47, that it was licensed as a morgue. The pub's history, as retold on its website (droppingwell.com), paints a picture of those dark days:

> Dublin was then a city beleaguered by dysentery, typhus, dropsy and fever as huddled, swarming masses of emaciated looking creatures left a ghostly trail across the land. Many were Dublin people themselves, while others arrived from the rest of the country in search of food, employment and shelter … The greatest tragedy of these starving masses lay not in the shortage of food, as hundreds of tons of corn and other food products left Irish ports each day, but in the hopeless destitution of a people who could not help themselves.

The Community Morgue and a Liquor Licence

Throughout Black '47, corpses of the unfortunate found their way into the Dodder, and the authorities were tasked with the difficult job of curtailing disease as much as possible and identifying the deceased before burial in mass graves. And so, when John Howe and his wife applied for a liquor licence at the site, their prime concern was helping in this effort. The request was granted and the Dropping Well opened for business in July 1847. It was a working public house but also somewhere that the deceased could be kept in a more dignified manner.

Sadly, Howe's exposure to these afflicted bodies took its toll; he fell ill and died in 1850. Mrs Howe continued to operate the pub for five years, before passing it on to a relative called Miss Williams.

The Boxer Meagher and a Lavish Renovation

In 1908, the pub was bought by P.H Meagher, who gave the premises a lavish makeover. Meagher was something of a legend in Dublin publican circles. He was passionate about sport, particularly boxing, which he dabbled in it in his earlier days, and he even erected a ring in the pub. Of course, boxing also came in handy when he had to enforce the strict rules he set down for his establishment. The present-day management boasts that Meagher gave the Dropping Well the reputation of 'the most orderly pub in Dublin' and today, 'the Boxer' is memorialised in the traditional bar, which Charlie Chawke named in his honour.

The Holy Hour and Drunks' Bona Fides

People working in the mills were paid on a Saturday after lunch; many went straight to the local pubs and stayed till closing time. Minister for Justice Kevin O'Higgins was concerned about this practice and was determined to do something about it. As the Dropping Well's website explains:

> Some months later in 1926 the Intoxicating Liquor Act came before the house and was passed into law accompanied by the provision of mandatory closing of public houses between 2.30 and 3.30 p.m. each day. In a very short time this piece of legislation entered the rich culture of Irish pub lore as the 'Holy Hour' and caused more infringements of the law than any other piece of legislation ever placed on the Irish statue [sic] books ... It eventually disappeared from the statue books in 1988.

The Goat, the Widow, the Lamb and the Dead Man's Inn

The Dropping Well meanwhile had managed to escape the provisions of the Act, using an archaic legal loophole. It stated that 'bone fide' travellers, that is, people 3 miles from their home (5 miles in Dublin), were allowed to drink alcohol outside standard hours. The excellent Dublin blog *Come Here to Me!* explains:

> There was at least one 'bona-fide' on each main road out of Dublin. They included Lamb Doyle's (Dublin Mountains), Widow Flavin's (Sandyford), the Dropping Well (Dartry), the Deadman's Inn (Lucan), the Swiss Cottage (Santry), the Igo Inn (Ballybrack) and The Goat (Goatstown).

The loophole was abolished in 1960.

Since 1847, the Dropping Well has enjoyed eight different landlords: Mr & Mrs John Howe, Miss Williams, Joseph Brownrigg, John Maher, Edward Daly, P.H. Meagher, the Cleary Family and the current owner, well-known Dublin publican Charlie Chawke.

From John Gray to William Martin Murphy – The Freeman's Journal

Long-time resident of Clareville House on Dartry Road was John Gray (1816–75), the controversial owner of the *Freeman's Journal*. He was a doctor, was indicted for conspiracy in 1843, knighted in 1863, was an MP for Kilkenny in 1865–75, and his statue resides to this day in Dublin's O'Connell Street. The statue commemorates his involvement in bringing Vartry Reservoir water into Dublin city and particularly to the Rathmines residents, for whom the water issue was the bane of their lives for decades. Interestingly, his successor as owner of the *Freeman's Journal* (later called *The Irish Independent*) was a Rathgar neighbour, William Martin Murphy, who lived at Orwell Park beside Dartry Road. Gray had also lived on Charleville Road, Rathmines, at Charleville House, where his wife, Lady Gray, died in 1887. This house later became part of St Louis Convent and Secondary School.

17

MEMORIES FROM THE CORRIDORS OF TIME

Rathmines is full of stories and memories. People still talk about 'the Chains', 'the bedsits of Flatland', beanbags from the Blackberry Market, dancing in St Joseph's Hall or the Leinster Cricket Club, the pubs including Slattery's, the Rathmines Inn, Madigan's or O'Byrne's. Others remember Hollyfield or Mount Pleasant Buildings, 'the Flea House' as the Stella Cinema was affectionately known in latter days, or the 'Prinner Cinema' nearly opposite the huge green-domed church with its Folk Mass on a Sunday evening.

Each one of us that grew up in the area or spent some time there will have our own reminiscences. Flat-dwellers who came from the four corners of Ireland will doubtless have many stories to tell. Former youngsters will recall playing amidst the ruins of the declining splendour of 'Lordy's', the former home of Lord and Lady Longford on Leinster Road, before it was requisitioned by developers! Or 'boxing the fox' in many of the local orchards. Or playing football on 'Buck's Lane' (Grosvenor Lane).

One of the Doran brothers, of the famous Doran's Barbershop on Castlewood Avenue, once upon a time recalled seeing former Taoiseach, Séan Lemass, regularly strolling along Castlewood Avenue from his home on Palmerston Road, on his way to the Stella Cinema, on a Saturday night. Doran's itself was legendary, giving 'short back and sides' and much else since 1913, despite the 'hippy' long-hair interlude of the 1960s and 1970s.

ORANGE MAIDS AND WOODBINES

Cinemagoers visiting the Stella would recall buying a couple of Orange Maids, or a packet of Sobraine Black Russian cigarettes in Harvey's tobacconist next door, or perhaps five Woodbines. Other old shops include Dorney's, Mahon's Dairy, Shaw's the hardware merchant (and of course Lenihan's Hardware), Miss Doorly's Sweet Shop and Cradock's Newsagent opposite the Garda Station. Nolan's Butchers (1936) was in business for more than eighty years until 2017. An original messenger boy's bike adorned the shop window. Likewise, with Deveney's off-licence near the Post Office which only ceased trading c.2015. It was in business since 1910, but now dispensing a different kind of drug from alcohol – medicines! And on a Saturday evening there would be queues of people waiting outside Cleggs on Lower Rathmines for their shoe repairs so they could be well shod for Sunday Mass!

RED SHOES, DUMBBELLS AND BARBELLS

People still talk about the Red Shoes cafe that used to only open in the evenings. It was in Swanville, just around the corner from the Stella. There is still a secret passage that leads from here to Prince Arthur Terrace and the back of Leinster Square, beloved by adventurous children. Another cafe was the Cope, with its jukebox. O'Keefe's, a family business long established in Rathmines, is still excellent for school uniforms, chess sets, snooker cues, dartboards, penknives and other sundry games and sports gear, not to mention their treasure trove of backgammon sets, lenser torches, dominoes, tooks, tennis rackets, dumbbells, barbells, the list goes on! There is no other shop like it!

FROM SLATTERY'S TO RODY BOLAND'S

Slattery's: with its unique snug accessed by the front hall door. The confessional-type window halfway along the hall is for putting in orders for drinks from those that prefer a little solitude or respite from the raucous bar inside. Rody Boland's (dating from 1873, although strictly speaking this date refers to its original incarnation in Nenagh, Co. Tipperary, where one Edward Boland opened his pub), the Corrigan's/Mount Pleasant Inn, the Grove Inn (now gone), O'Byrne's (now Grace's) and Madigan's Pub (now Copan's Pub with the date 1843 and the original name of Leinster House carved in mosaic high above the entrance) are amongst others that are fondly remembered.

The Swan Centre, deriving its name from the River Swan, has some terrific long-term family businesses including The Hopsack, Dubray Bookshop, The Kylemore and Alan Hanna's Bookshop. The Blindcraft Shop across from the green-domed church was the workplace for many years of the visually disabled who made their living from weaving baskets and many other useful wicker-based items.

FROM SNOOKER TO THE BLACKBERRY MARKET

The Rathmines Snooker Hall on Upper Rathmines Road (later the Zen Chinese Restaurant) evokes memories for many. So you would not get too cold playing snooker, they used to provide hot water and a small sachet of some strange powder for your instant cup of soup! Any many students recall buying their first beanbag at the Blackberry Market, next door to Rathmines Church. Not forgetting the Herman Wilkinson Auction Rooms from where many a flat or bedsit were (and continue to be!) furnished. It is, in the company's own words, 'the last of the traditional auction rooms, with a wide variety of specialist auctions in addition to Dublin's famous weekly household and furniture auction. These rooms have been continuously a feature of the Rathmines and Dublin commercial landscape since 1928.' They hold between eighty and ninety auctions every year, more than any other auction rooms in Ireland.

ARMADA PAPERBACKS FOR BOYS AND GIRLS

The Banba Bookshop along by the Town Hall was for many years a landmark bookshop trading in second-hand paperback books – a great boon to the voracious reading habits of children! Armada Paperbacks for Boys and Girls was a by-word for happiness! They were usually originally priced at *2s/6d* (a half a crown, or two and six in the old pre-decimal money) but we bought them for a few pennies!

OF LAUNDRIES, HANDKERCHIEFS AND CROSS FACES ON CATS

Although the building is gone, save for the facade fronting a block of apartments, the staff of Kelso Laundry on Lower Rathmines Road are remembered by a tree (called the Handkerchief Tree) in nearby Harold's Cross Park for their heroic and successful struggle for better working conditions for laundry staff in the 1940s. Some will recall the Swastika-emblazoned laundry vans in the area.

The old swimming pool up Williams Place (with its terrace of mid-nineteenth-century four-storey houses) is now replaced with the new Swan Leisure Centre. It is very impressive inside with the wall murals and is reminiscent of the old Turkish bath houses in Dublin. The seating outside, mind you, would put a cross face on a cat! Instead of slats on the benches going from east to west or left to right, they are laid north to south, inviting the most excruciating consequences for the unwary and tired traveller.

MEETING AT THE MET AND BURLESQUE AMBIANCE

The Swan Shopping Centre now has a new multi-cinema complex built overhead. It is the first cinema in Dublin custom designed for digital cinema. Here you can listen and watch, live, the opera beamed in from the Met or some of the world's great opera houses.

The old Stella Cinema has been revived and returned to its former glory with a stylish interior including its restored decorative ceiling and with a burlesque-luxe ambiance. Blockbusters and art-house films are on the menu.

BOOKS, BOOKS AND MORE BOOKS! A DOG'S LIFE FOR MOLLY AND TIGGER

Dubray's Bookshop, the Bookstation and Alan Hanna's Bookshop are also favourites with the local residents. The friendly and unfailingly helpful staff makes visiting these bookshops a pleasure. Each has its own unique identity and personality. The former is part of a family-run enterprise, and the Rathmines branch is run under the very capable and expert hands of the manageress, Aileen Smyth, as well as Vivienne and the staff. A lovely, friendly and happy bookshop – and not forgetting their November 'Author's Night'! Alan Hanna's Bookshop, a long-established and highly respected family business, has its own dog in residence to welcome browsers! Molly the dog took early retirement and was soon replaced by Tigger! This gem of a shop, with the ever-helpful Kevin, Charles et al, is easy to miss, squeezed in between the former Ulster Bank and Burdock's Chipper on Lower Rathmines Road. This is a real bookshop, with shelves stacked to the rafters with books. It's always a pleasure to haphazardly navigate your way through mountains of new and second-hand volumes, and these are piled high in various corners of the long, narrow shop, meaning that most of the limited floor space is taken up by books and books ... and more books. What more could you ask for? Yes, a coffee and bun in the classic, bookcovers-festooned little Bark cafe! Hanna's is a friendly, independent Irish store that has kept its own identity – certainly one to be celebrated. And always a hive of activity. A real treasure in Rathmines!

THE HOPSACK FOR THE ULTIMATE SOURCE OF LIFE

And for the health-conscious, another family-run business, the Hopsack healthfood store in the Swan Centre, is well worth a visit. Here you will find everything you would need, including Ultimate Magnesium, Source of Life Gold, Rosehip Oil, Salad Blue Potatoes, Good Green Stuff, Org Raw Coconut Oil, Nutrient Plus Firming Serum and NuMe Botanical Cleansing Support, not forgetting organic fruit, vegetables and an excellent salad bar. And of course, the tasty Banana Man shake. Here you will meet the streamlined Finn, doubtless a descendant of him with the same name, who was renowned as a hunter-warrior in Irish mythology. It is the modern-day Finn who is still the hunter, but of a different kind, and is consequently possessed by an encyclopaedic knowledge of all things healthy. His extraordinary knowledge, combined with good business acumen and strong customer loyalty, makes this emporium a veritable institution in Rathmines. Long may this family business thrive in Rathmines.

RATHMINES STYLE FOR BUDDING WRITERS AND MUSICIANS

The old College of Commerce is now a college of the Dublin Institute of Technology (DIT) and has expanded to include a School of Journalism. The *Rathmines Style Book* is a must for budding journalists. Well-known journalist and author Louis McRedmond became the first director of the course in journalism in Rathmines in 1970. The words, 'The Rathmines Technical Institute' are still plainly visible on the Leinster Road side of the building, around the corner from the entrance to Rathmines Library, and it is now the home of the DIT College of Music. You will often hear the sweet tones of budding singers and musicians wafting out on a breeze from the top windows as you pass this fine building.

THE NOBEL PRIZE WINNER AND THE LIVELY LEPRECHAUN

The Central Statistics Office occupies a large office building on Ardee Road, near the entrance to Cathal Brugha Barracks. Established in 1949 as the country's national statistics office, the CSO, in the organisation's own words, 'meets the needs of Government for quality statistical information, which is vital for the formation, implementation and monitoring of policy and programmes at national, regional and local levels in a rapidly changing economic and social environment'. It came to international prominence in recent years over its statistics on the fast-growing Irish economy – its figures seemed to show a 26 per cent spurt of growth in GDP (figures skewed by the presence of multinational companies such as aircraft leasing companies) which was at odds with the economic realities. It quickly addressed the analysis to give us more sober statistics (approximately 4 per cent growth per anum.) using a new measure of economic growth. It was Paul Krugmann, the Nobel Prize winning economist who allegedly coined the term 'leprechaun economics' in response to the inflated figures. It's no wonder he won the prize.

FROM THE RATHMINES RIOT TO BEANBAGS AND BAUBLES

Rathmines forges all kinds of memories for past and present residents. Who recalls the riots in Rathmines in the mid 1930s when CYMS Catholic Action activists clashed with those attending a Communist meeting in the Town Hall? It got huge coverage in the newspapers of the time as fears of Communist infiltration was taken very seriously by some. Or who recalls Thin Lizzy's Phil Lynott attending the College of Commerce? Or the trams going up and down Rathmines Road? Or the burning down of Rathmines Catholic Church? Some might recall the familiar figure of Lord Longford as he made his way down Leinster Road on his way to The Gate. Or the chain-smoking bespectacled Fr Michael Cleary with the newspapers clasped under his arm as he sauntered around Rathmines and Harold's

IRISH CHRISTIAN FRONT

A Public Meeting

WILL BE HELD AT

RATHMINES TOWN HALL

ON

Saturday, 14TH November, 1936

AT 8 P.M.

To form a Branch of the
IRISH CHRISTIAN FRONT in
the Rathmines and Rathgar area.
Prominent Speakers will address
the Meeting.

Show by your presence at this Meeting that
Ireland Rejects Communism

Powell Press, Dublin.

1930s Ireland, when fears about Communism were a major issue. Rathmines Town Hall was the location of a violent clash between CYMS/ICF Catholic Actionists and Communists on one occasion during the 1930s when the latter also held a meeting in the Town Hall.

Cross on a Sunday morning. Not forgetting the Blackberry Market (opposite Blackberry Lane) with its plethora of beanbags and every imaginable book and bauble and which concocted images of the Orient, right here in the heart of Rathmines.

CAKES, GUINNESS AND THE FCA

Or who remembers Ferguson's cake shop and tearooms, located where the Swan Centre now is. Although it was called Ferguson's, an Austrian family owned it. The Austrians were known for their cake-making and pastries at the time. Even then there were different nationalities living and working in Rathmines. We also remember pounding the Cathal Brugha Barracks square on a Sunday morning with the Free Clothes Association, as the FCA part-time army was affectionately called.

THE LIVE MIKE AND THE BOUNCING CHEQUE

In the years 1979–82, RTÉ's Mike Murphy was a familiar figure around Rathmines. As part of his 'candid camera' pranks he disguised himself and tried to pull the wool over people's eyes by persuading people to let him into their houses, or persuading them to give him a loan of a bike or a car etc., pretending he was someone of importance. All sorts of devilment, in fact! He grew up in the area and this doubtlessly inspired him to launch his brand of humour, *The Live Mike*, on the unsuspecting and at times horrified residents. The candid camera scenes invariably ended with the host saying, 'I'm Mike Murphy from RTÉ'. One senior citizen was heard to tell him: 'If ya don't get away from me, ye aul hare baiter, I'll blow your brains out with me brolly!' Another warned him: 'Get up the yard, there's a smell of Benjy off ya!'

On another occasion, he asked long-time resident of Rathmines (Neville Road and Cowper Village), Annie Kavanagh, if 'he could go home with her'. 'Off with you,' she said, 'sure haven't I somebody already at home to look after' (her husband Joe). Mrs Kavanagh herself went on to make history by being, at the age of 102, reputedly the oldest resident of Rathmines, of Dublin, and one of the oldest people in Ireland. She was still mobile at the age of 100 and was happy to receive a cheque from President Mary McAleese on reaching the centenary. 'Let's hope it doesn't bounce!' she quipped, rushing into the bank.

LIARS AND CONFESSIONALS

The following is a story told by Mike Murphy himself and gives an interesting snapshot into another era and way of life:

So anyway, I had to go to confession and I had a few goodies to tell because I wasn't the best behaved at a certain stage in my life. I decided that I better not go to my own parish where the priest would know me so I went down to Rathmines instead. At the time, I had got on the radio alright – I was doing stuff in the evening on RTÉ. So, I told the priest this whopper of a one that I had and he gave me absolution and 'God Bless you.' I was just getting up to go and he said, 'Just a moment my son – that wouldn't be a familiar voice I hear?' So I froze. 'How do you mean, Father?' He says, 'That wouldn't be Tony Lyons, the news reader, would it?' I said, 'It would, Father' … Then I had to go to confession on the other side of the church because I just told a lie.

THE ARCHER AND FORD CONNECTION

Some may also remember Archers Garage on Upper Rathmines Road owned by R.W. Archer, a pioneer in the motor trade, and who had a special relationship with Henry Ford (1st) and the Ford Motor Company in Cork. In 1907, Ford made its debut in Ireland, at the Irish Motor Show at the RDS. Three Model N's were exhibited, and Mr Archer signed the very first Irish sales contract for Ford at the show. Archer was clearly impressed with the cars, but he did not find them an easy sell at first, as the brand was relatively unknown. In time, however, word began to spread, thanks in part to the Model N winning gold in the 1907 and '08 Irish Reliability Trials. By the time the Model T was launched, there was a captive audience and it was an immediate success. According to the Central Statistics Office, by 1913, 600 Fords had been sold in Ireland. And Rathmines residents played no insignificant part in the Ford success story.

FURTHER READING

Ball, F.E., *A History of the County Dublin* (Alexander Thom: Dublin, 1902–17).

Barry, Michael, *Victorian Dublin Revealed* (Andalus Press: Dublin, 2011).

Connell, Joseph, *Dublin Rising 1916* (Dublin: Wordwell, 2015).

Curtis, Maurice, *Rathmines. Ireland in Old Photographs* (Dublin: The History Press Ireland, 2011).

Curtis, Maurice, *Portobello* (Dublin: The History Press Ireland, 2012).

Curtis, Maurice, *The Liberties: A History* (Dublin: The History Press Ireland, 2013).

Curtis, Maurice, *Glasnevin* (Dublin: The History Press Ireland, 2014).

Curtis, Maurice, *Rathfarnham* (Dublin: The History Press Ireland, 2014).

Curtis, Maurice, *To Hell or Monto. Dublin's Two Most Notorious Districts* (Dublin: The History Press Ireland, 2015).

Curtis, Maurice, *Temple Bar. A History* (Dublin: The History Press Ireland, 2016).

Curtis, Maurice, *Rathgar: A History* (Dublin: The History Press Ireland, 2016).

Curtis, Maurice, *The Little Book of Ranelagh* (Dublin: The History Press Ireland, 2017).

Curtis, Maurice, *Playing with Skulls. A Dublin Childhood* (Dublin: The Liffey Press, 2017).

Curtis, Maurice, *The Liberties in Pictures* (Dublin: Currach Press, 2018).

Daly, Ita, *We Were Happy Here. A History of St Louis School* (Dublin: St Louis School, 2014).

Daly, Mary; Hearn, Mona; Pearson, Peter, *Dublin's Victorian Houses* (Dublin: A&A Farmar, 1998).

Donnelly, N., *A Short History of the Parishes of Dublin* (CTSI: Dublin, 1900).

Gilbert, J.T., *A History of the City of Dublin* 3 Volumes (Gill & MacMillan: Dublin, 1978).

Handcock, William Domville, *The History and Antiquities of Tallaght n The County of Dublin* (Figgis: Dublin: 2nd Edition, 1877).

Hayes-McCoy, G.A., *Irish Battles: A Military History of Ireland* (Irish Books & Media: Dublin, 1998).

Joyce, Weston St. John, *The Neighbourhood of Dublin* (Skellig: Dublin, 1988).

Kavanagh, Ray, *Mamie Cadden: Backstreet Abortionist* (Mercier Press: Cork, 2005).

Kearns, George, *The Prinner: The Story of the Princess Cinema Rathmines and Other Dublin Picture Palaces and Cinemas* (George P. Kearns: Dublin, 2005).

Kearns, George & Maguire, Patrick, *A-Z of All Old Dublin Cinemas* (George P. Kearns: Dublin, 2007).

Keenan, Jim, *Dublin Cinemas* (Picture House Publications: Dublin, 2005).

Kelly, Deirdre, *Four Roads. The History of Rathmines, Ranelagh and Leeson Street* (The O'Brien Press: Dublin, 1995).

Lewis, Samuel, *Lewis's Topographical Dictionary of Ireland* (S. Lewis & Co.: London, 1837).

MacDevitt, Murrough, *Centenary Book of The Leinster Cricket Club* (LCC: Dublin, 2002).

MacThomáis, Eamonn, *Me Jewel and Darling Dublin* 20th Anniversary Edition. (Dublin: The O'Brien Press, 1998).

Marreco, Anne, *The Rebel Countess. The Life and Times of Constance Markievicz* (Orion: London, 2002).

O'Maitiú. Séamus, *Dublin's Suburban Towns 1834–1930* (Four Courts Press: Dublin, 2002).

Quinlan, Carmel, *Genteel Revolutionaries: Anna and Thomas Haslam and the Irish Women's Movement* (Cork: UCC. 2005).

Rockett, Kevin with Rockett, Emer, *Film Exhibition and Distribution in Ireland, 1909–2010* (Four Courts Press: Dublin, 2011).

Royal Irish Academy, *Dictionary of Irish Biography* (Cambridge: Cambridge University Press, 2009).

Zimmermann, Marc, *A History of Dublin Cinemas* (Nonsuch Publishing: Dublin, 2007).